D1236519

THE OPERATIC QUIZ BOOK

Also by James Camner:

The Great Composers in Historic Photographs, Dover, 1981

The Great Instrumentalists in Historic Photographs, Dover, 1980

The Great Opera Stars in Historic Photographs, Dover, 1979

How to Enjoy Opera, Doubleday & Co., 1981

Stars of the American Musical Theater in Historic Photographs. (with Stanley Appelbaum), Dover, 1981

James Camner

THE OPERATIC QUIZ BOOK

St. Martin's Press • New York

Copyright © 1982 by James Camner
For information, write: St. Martin's Press,
175 Fifth Avenue, New York, N.Y. 10010
Manufactured in the United States of America

Library of Congress Cataloging in Publication Data

Camner, James.
    The operatic quiz book.

    1. Opera I. Title.
ML1700.C185   782.1   81-18203
ISBN 0-312-58678-7   AACR2

Design by Ed Kaplin

10 9 8 7 6 5 4 3 2 1

First Edition

Most of the rare illustrations in this book first
appeared in *Harper's Weekly* in the 19th century.
To these we added two "Gibson Girls" by Charles Dana Gibson
and an old Victrola ad for Caruso records.

This book is dedicated to my father, Irwin D. Camner.

ACKNOWLEDGMENTS

Despite my incredible store of opera trivia, which has so often been a burden to my friends and family, this amazing compilation wouldn't have been possible without help from the following: Tony Randall, Anna Sosenko, Robert Tollett, Stanley Appelbaum, Jan Peerce, Risë Stevens and Lim Lai, who sent in questions; Bismarck Reine, Richard Arsenty, Martin Sokol, Jordan Massee, Howard and Paola Greenfeld, Robert Merrill, Robert Tuggle and Charles Hamilton, whose suggestions became questions in this book; my wonderful copyist, Cherryl Lurtsema; and my editor, Ashton Applewhite. Finally, this book would have been impossible without the invaluable assistance of my wife, Connie.

James Camner

Drawing by George Wolfe Plank

IN THE GOLDEN HORSESHOE

THE OPENING NIGHT OF THE METROPOLITAN OPERA HOUSE, NOVEMBER 17, 1913

(*Drawn by one of "Lighter Vein's" younger and more impressionable artists*)

THE OPERATIC QUIZ BOOK

CONTENTS

CHRISTINE NILSSON'S LAST NIGHT AT DRURY LANE

OVERTURE

How much do you know about opera?

Here is a book that will challenge your credentials. Most people qualify as opera experts after seeing one live performance; at least that seems to be enough to start them talking as if they were.

And why not? Opera, after all, is entertainment, and everyone knows what he likes. But if the reader can't answer the question sent in to us by Tony Randall, the popular actor and opera authority, perhaps a little more study is in order. A number of opera stars and scholars have contributed questions for this book, but his is the essential first one. He wrote:

> Dear Mr. Camner,
> The only question that comes to mind
> is Boris Goldovsky's favorite:
> Name three operas.

If you can answer that one, rest assured that many of the questions in the book will be within your grasp.

In order to make the book more challenging, we have arranged a point system. At the end of every question, the possible points or combination of points is contained in parentheses. At the end of each Answers section is space in which to note your score. If no other instructions are given, then the question must be answered in full to obtain the points. Many questions have two or more parts, and it will be possible to accumulate points on questions you may only partially know the answers to. On the last page, you'll see how you rate according to our evaluation. Good luck!

MADAME CHRISTINE NILSSON.—Photographed by Sarony.

MADAME ADELINA PATTI.—Photographed by Sarony.

MADAME ETELKA GERSTER.—Photographed by Falk.

MADAME MARCELLA SEMBRICH.—Photographed by Mora.

ACT I

Superstar Trivia

We begin our quiz book with questions about famous opera stars. Here you'll find out how much you know about your favorite singers. Logically, we begin with the most celebrated singer of the century, Enrico Caruso.

Answers on p. 18.

Scene One: Caruso

A Very Good Year

1. The year 1873 has been called by opera devotees the Annus Mirabilis because, along with Caruso, many other great singers were born in that year. Take 10 points if you can name seven of them. (10)

2. Where was Caruso born (country and town)? (1)

3. What was Caruso's most unsuccessful performance at the Metropolitan Opera? (2)

4. Name the six world premieres Caruso participated in. (2 points for each, for a total of 12)

5. Caruso was only thirty when he made his debut at:

(a) La Scala

(b) The Metropolitan Opera

(c) Covent Garden

(d) Teatro San Carlo

(e) The Bolshoi

(1)

6. Although Caruso is said to have brought the house down many times when he sang, there was one time when the house actually did collapse after he performed. Take 2 points if you can name the opera he sang and another 2 if you can explain why the house fell down. (4)

Caruso's Only Flop

7. One thing Caruso wasn't was a movie actor. What was the name of the movie he starred in? (2)

8. How did Caruso obtain his release from the Italian army? (4)

9. What Caruso performance was canceled due to a bombing, and where? (4)

10. What was the last opera Caruso sang? (3)

11. Although it is now common practice for popular songs to receive their first performance on a recording, Caruso was one of the first singers to record a "premiere." Can you name a song that is still performed of which Caruso gave the very first performance when he recorded it? (3)

12. Caruso was given many decorations by Italy, France, England and Germany, including the Crown of Italy, the Legion of Honor, the Order of British Victoria and the Order of Crown Eagle of Prussia. How many decorations were awarded to Caruso by the United States? (4)

13. What Met performance by Caruso earned him no more applause than the amount usually received by a *comprimario*? (2)

14. When he was asked, "How is the King of Tenors today?" Enrico Caruso replied, "Since when have you become a bass?" To whom was he speaking? (1)

15. What connection did the bandleader Xavier Cugat have with Caruso? (3)

16. Caruso amused himself and his friends with witty and sometimes wicked caricatures of famous people. What famous bass was also noted for his caricatures? (2)

Among the singers in recent years who have received adulation comparable to that of Caruso are Luciano Pavarotti, Maria Callas and Beverly Sills. These stars are so familiar to the public that it was difficult to find little-known facts about them. The following, however, should challenge even their most ardent fans.

Scene Two: Pavarotti

17. Where was Luciano Pavarotti born (country and town)? (2)

18. Who was the first famous tenor Pavarotti heard in person? (3)

19. Who was the first tenor Pavarotti heard in person? (1)

20. While he was a vocal student, Pavarotti held down two different jobs. What were they? (2 points for each, for a total of 4)

21. Name Pavarotti's two main singing instructors. (3 points for each, for a total of 6)

22. What other singer who later became famous studied with one of Pavarotti's teachers? (1)

23. Rodolfo in *La Bohème* has played an important part in Pavarotti's career. Where and when were the four important debuts Pavarotti made in that role? (2 points for each, for a total of 8)

24. In what role and where did Pavarotti make his debut in the United States? (3)

25. Name the famous tenor who was Pavarotti's first manager. (4)

26. Pavarotti has sung all but one of the following onstage. Which role? (2)

Idamante in *Idomeneo*
Canio in *Pagliacci*

Oronte in *I Lombardi*
Italian Singer in *Der Rosenkavalier*

Scene Three: Callas

27. (a) What opera served for Maria Callas's debut in Italy in 1947? (3)

(b) What role did Callas sing for her very first performance of an opera? (4)

28. What are the four roles Callas recorded but never sang onstage? (6)

29. For a prima donna, the greatest sin a partner in a duet can commit is to hold a note longer than she does. At the Met one baritone dared the wrath of Maria Callas and informed her that she could not sustain the note properly! The Met quickly fired him. Who was this brave, if foolish, baritone? (3)

30. This question was sent to us by Robert Tollett of New

York City: What did Maria Callas request as a substitute for the flowers lavished on her by an adoring fan? (10)

Scene Four: Sills

31. What is Beverly Sills's given name and what is her famous nickname? (4)

32. Who was Beverly Sills's teacher? (2)

33. Name four other women besides Beverly Sills who have run opera companies. (10)

34. What is the name of the movie in which Beverly Sills appeared? (5)

35. Take 5 points if you can name two of the three radio shows Beverly Sills appeared on as a regular. (5)

36. Queen of the New York City Opera, Beverly Sills has been noted for her portrayal of opera queens. We came up with seven queens that she has sung onstage. Name six. (8)

37. Beverly Sills made her grand-opera debut as Frasquita in *Carmen* with what company? (2)

38. Beverly Sills's first leading part in grand opera was with the Charles Wagner Touring Company in 1951. What was this part? (2)

39. In what role did Beverly Sills first appear at the New York City Opera in 1955? (2)

The following questions feature a cast of stars that opera lovers can only dream about, composed of the superstars throughout the history of opera. Hint: Some of the answers may include the four singers covered in questions 1 through 39.

Scene Five: A Galaxy of Stars

40. What did the great soprano Adelina Patti mean when she sent this message: "I have one shoe on!" (3)

41. What future famous Otello began his Met career as the Messenger in *Aida?* (2)

42. What soprano sang the first coloratura roulades? (9)

43. Who was the singer who was told by his teacher to give up because his voice was "lost in the wind"? (2)

44. Some singers just can't seem to live without other singers. Each of the following was married to another famous singer. Name their spouses. (1 point for each correct answer, for a total of 8)
(a) Ernest Nicolini
(b) Paul Kalisch
(c) Giulia Grisi
(d) Walter Berry
(e) Thomas Stewart
(f) Bidu Sayão
(g) George Chehanovsky
(h) Sandra Warfield

45. Who was the first black singer at the Met? (1)

46. Why were *castrati* (castrated men with soprano voices) introduced into opera? (3)

47. Soprano rivalries began to heat up early in the opera game. Can you name the first celebrated sopranos to feud with each other? (3)

One Drink Too Many?

48. A famous tenor was making a recording of the love duet from *Madame Butterfly* when the soprano smelled liquor on his breath. She sang the words, "He had a highball," instead of, *"Si per la vita."* Who were the tenor and the soprano? (2)

49. Who was the most exalted personage (politically) ever to participate in an opera performance? (3)

50. Another exalted personage was the fabulous Lilli Lehmann. How many roles did this titanic soprano sing in opera? (5)

Instrumental Divertissements

51. (a) What famous pianist also had a good career as an opera singer? (2)
    (b) What famous singer began as a potential concert pianist? (2)
    (c) What famous singer of today is a fine violinist? (1)
    (d) What legendary singer was considered equally expert on violin and piano? (1)

52. What tenor had the most famous high C during the second decade of the twentieth century? (3)

53. Many singers have had dishes named after them. We found several. Can you name three of the most famous? (5)

54. This question was sent in by Anna Sosenko, a noted theater producer and antiquarian bookseller: What fat singer was called an "elephant that swallowed a nightingale"? Who was the author of this witticism? (2 points for each part, for a total of 4)

55. Sometimes you hear that singers and conductors don't get along. But you wouldn't know it from the many times they have collaborated—on marriage! Name the conductor-husbands of the following singers:

(a) Pauline de Ahna   (e) Joan Sutherland
(b) Lucille Marcel   (f) Meta Seinemeyer
(c) Auguste Seidl-Kraus   (g) Lily Pons
(d) Marilyn Horne

(1 point for each correct match, for a possible total of 7 points)

56. (a) What singer retired from opera to sing the same four songs every night for ten years to an eccentric monarch?
(b) Who was the monarch?
(4 points for each part, for a total of 8)

57. What "silver-voiced tenor" was the first "king" of Italian opera in America? Name his successor. (3 points for each, for a total of 6)

58. Who was P. T. Barnum's "Swedish Nightingale"? (1)

59. Who were two other "Swedish Nightingales"? (6)

60. Who said, "What time's the next swan?" and why? (1)

Prima Donnas

61. Who were the prima donnas who sang in the premiere performances at:
(a) the Paris Opéra in 1875 (the present building)
(b) the Vienna Court Opera in 1869
(c) the Metropolitan Opera in 1883
(d) the Metropolitan Opera at Lincoln Center in 1966
(Take 2 points for each prima donna, for a total of 8)

62. What was Rosa Ponselle's middle name? (2)

63. While she was on her first tour in New York, what famous soprano appeared as a soloist at historic Grace Church? (6)

64. (a) What cantor of the early 1900s was celebrated enough to sing at the Met in Sunday concert performances, although he resisted offers to perform in opera?
   (b) Name two famous cantors who did sing opera at the Met.
(2 points for (a) and 2 points for the complete answer to (b), for a total of 4)

65. Although she was born shortly after her mother sang a performance of *Norma*, this diva never sang the role. Name her. (3)

66. Two famous quartets dominated the Age of Bel Canto: the *Puritani* and *Pasquale* quartets, the four leading singers in the first performances of *I Puritani* and *Don Pasquale*. Both quartets were identical except for one singer. Name the five singers that made up the two quartets. (5)

67. What American singer was so admired by Gustav Mahler that she sang the first performance of *Das Lied von der Erde* under his baton? (3)

68. Everyone knows that Caruso was the most famous tenor to record in the early days of recording. At that same time, who was the most famous tenor not to record? (1)

69. Who was the first tenor to sing a high C from the chest? (2)

70. What soprano had such a glorious six-year career that her name became a synonym for "dramatic soprano"? (3)

71. Did you know that the first American singer to achieve celebrity was the first woman elected to the Hall of Fame? Name her. (3)

72. Placido Domingo made his American debut opposite a legendary diva in her last performance in opera. For 2 points each: (a) Where? (b) In what opera? (c) Who was the soprano? (6)

73. Ten famous sopranos were pupils of the pedagogue Mathilde Marchesi. Name six for 5 points. (5)

74. A "mad" New York City hatter named John Genin once paid $275 for a ticket to a concert given by whom? (2)

75. Although the Metropolitan Opera waited until 1955 to hire a black singer, a full-blooded Indian chief had earlier starred in baritone roles like Scarpia in *Tosca*, and, with curious ethnic logic, in the title role of *The Polish Jew* in 1921. Who was the chief? (8)

76. Who was the shortest Aida? (5)

77. What prima donna took curtain calls with a goose under her arm? (1)

78. What diva's husband disappeared while flying in a balloon over the English Channel? (3)

79. In what country was the creator of the exotic title role in *Lakmé* born? (2)

The Death Bounce

80. What Rachel in *La Juive* was lucky enough to bounce

back up upon being thrown into the caldron of "boiling oil"?
(5)

81. Who was the first to sing Carmen in America and England? (3)

82. What singer sang Carmen in Swedish at the Met? (3)

83. Where did the superb Swedish tenor Jussi Bjoerling make his American debut? (3)

84. Many physically unattractive singers have succeeded on the stage because of their artistry, but none perhaps so signally as an Italian tenor who, though he was a hunchback, braved and vanquished the scorn of his audiences. It is said that at his Paris debut he advanced to the front of the stage before singing a note and asked the patrons to hold their jeers until he had begun to sing. Who was he? (7)

85. What opera singer wrote scenarios for ballets danced by Marie Taglioni and Fanny Elssler? (5)

86. Prima donnas have not had a reputation for high intelligence. It is known that Verdi considered them stupid, and Toscanini once grabbed a prominent part of a singer's anatomy, exclaiming, "If only these were brains!" However, this is a "bum rap." Most divas are quite intelligent, and some have even exhibited noteworthy literary talents.
(a) What prima donna published a book of her collected witticisms? (5)
(b) What prima donna wrote a play that was produced, in addition to a published novel and poetry? (5)
(c) What prima donna published a successful murder mystery? (1)

87. Who was the greatest opera singer ever born in Shanghai? (2)

88. Sobbing tenors are all too common today, but can you name the first tenor to use a sob? (2)

89. What leading international opera star is part Maori? (1)

90. The wonderful bass Ezio Pinza had one role that he liked most and one, surprisingly, that he disliked most. Name them for two points each. (4)

91. When you rang the doorbell at Ezio Pinza's house in Connecticut, what did you hear? (4)

92. Name two famous sopranos who died while on tour. (3 points for each, for a total of 6)

93. What great Wagnerian soprano once played the unlikely part of the *castrato* Farinelli in an opera? (3)

94. Opera singers have been called dogs, but what famous opera singer was named after one? (4)

95. While prima donnas have often forced opera managements to accept their husbands as singers or conductors, we found only one instance of a soprano forcing a cellist down management's throat. The diva was Theresa Förster, and the opera house was the Metropolitan. Can you name the cellist? (3)

96. This question was sent to us by opera historian Lim Lai: From the beginning of the twentieth century up to the first World War, there have been many American singers who had their early careers in Europe before their successes in the United States. Can you identify the following singers? (5 points for each, 15 total)
(a) Born 1878; died 1964. Noted soprano who sang leading roles with Caruso in Munich. Sang in Holland, London and later in New York. Created the role of Ariadne in the

Munich premiere of Richard Strauss's *Ariadne auf Naxos*.
(b) Born 1870; died 1954. Very important bass who was a great favorite at the Dresden Hofoper. Sang with the Damrosch-Ellis Opera Company, Bayreuth, Covent Garden and the Met. He sang in the first recording of a complete act of a Wagner opera: Act II of *Tannhäuser*, as the Landgraf.
(c) Important bass who sang leading roles at the Berlin Hofoper from 1906–1911. Also sang with Savage Opera Company and Metropolitan Opera. Besides Berlin, he also sang in Frankfurt and Munich. He died at the early age of 38 (February 26, 1914).

97. Many American singers have achieved great fame in the United States before ever going to Europe, if at all. Can you identify the following singers? (2 points for each, 6 total)
(a) Born 1842; died 1916. Claimed to be the first American prima donna (she was not the first or the last to make this claim). She was the first American singer to be acclaimed in Russia. Longfellow wrote that "She reminded me of Dryden's lines—'So pois'd, so gently she descends from high,/It seems a soft dismission from the sky.'"
(b) Tenor born May 29, 1892; died 1966. He sounded remarkably like Caruso and has been mistaken for him by record collectors. Made his Met debut in 1920, gaining prominence in eight seasons there. Later popular at the Opéra-Comique as Mârouf.
(c) Contralto born in St. Louis in 1897; died 1962. Discovered by Schumann-Heink. After one year of study she made her Met debut as the Italian Singer in *Manon Lescaut*. She made only one very famous recording for Victor and retired to marry the owner of Wells-Fargo.

98. This puzzler was sent in by one of the legendary singers of our time: What famous singer also answers to the names Jacob Pincus Perelmuth, Pinky Pearl, Jascha Pearl, Paul Robinson and Randolph Joyce? (2)

99. Here are some more name twisters:

(a) Kalogeropoulos was the given last name of a singer whose worldwide fame was acquired under what name? (1)

(b) What singer's stage name meant "Lily of the North"? (1)

(c) What soprano was known as the Minnesota Nightingale? (6)

(d) Emma Wixom took her stage name from a city near her birthplace. What was her famous name and where was the city? (3)

ACT I: Answers

Scene One: Caruso

1. Lillian Blauvelt, Feodor Chaliapin, Clara Butt, Andres de Segurola, Otto Goritz, Karl Jörn, Salomea Kruszelniski, Rose Olitzka, Marie Rappold, Leo Slezak, Alice Verlet and Herbert Witherspoon are the most famous.

2. Naples, Italy.

3. His most unsuccessful performance was unquestionably his first in New York, when he debuted on opening night, November 23, 1903, as the Duke in *Rigoletto*. Critical opinion was divided, with the *Tribune* complaining of his "tiresome Italian mannerisms."

4. *L'Arlesiana* by Cilea; November 27, 1897.
Fedora by Giordano; November 17, 1898.
Le Maschere by Mascagni (at La Scala, one of seven simultaneous premieres on the same date); January 17, 1901.
Germania by Franchetti; March 11, 1902.
Adriana Lecouvreur by Cilea; November 6, 1902.
La Fanciulla del West by Puccini; December 10, 1910.

5. (b) The Metropolitan Opera.

6. Caruso sang in *Carmen* on April 17, 1906, the night before the San Francisco Earthquake. He never sang in San Francisco again.

7. The disaster was *My Cousin,* a silent film, which probably explains why.

8. His brother, Giovanni, obligingly entered as a substitute.

9. *Aida* in Havana on June 13, 1920, was canceled due to an explosion meant for him set by extortionists.

10. *La Juive* on December 24, 1920, at the Metropolitan.

11. *Mattinata* by Leoncavallo was recorded in 1904, with the composer accompanying him.

12. None!

13. Just for fun, he once sang Beppe's offstage serenade in the second act of *Pagliacci*, receiving no more applause than is usually given to the singer of that aria. Perhaps he wanted to see if it was his voice or his looks that the audience went wild about!

14. John McCormack, a good friend whom Caruso greatly admired.

15. Xavier Cugat was Caruso's accompanist for some concerts.

16. Feodor Chaliapin, whose son Boris was the portrait painter for *Time* magazine.

Scene Two: Pavarotti

17. Modena, Italy.

18. Beniamino Gigli.

19. His father, Fernando, not a bad singer himself, has made some joint appearances with his famous son in recent years.

20. Pavarotti worked as an elementary-school teacher and as an insurance salesman.

21. Arrigo Pola and Ettore Campogalliani.

22. Mirella Freni also studied with Campogalliani.

23. At Reggio Emilia, April 28, 1961, his debut in opera.
At his Covent Garden debut, 1963.
At his San Francisco debut, 1967.
At his Met debut, 1968.

24. In Miami, Florida, as Edgardo in *Lucia* in 1965.

25. Alessandro Ziliani, a tenor who often sang with Toscanini.

26. As of the writing of this book, Pavarotti has never sung Canio onstage, although he has recorded it.

Scene Three: Callas

27. (a) *La Gioconda*
(b) Santuzza, in Athens, in 1938.

28. Mimi in *La Bohème;* Carmen; Manon Lescaut; Nedda in *Pagliacci*.

29. Enzo Sordello. It was at a 1956 performance of *Lucia* that he held his glorious high note too long for the good of his career.

30. Coat hangers! "Send me something useful for a change," commanded the diva.

Scene Four: Sills

31. Born Belle Miriam Silverman, "Bubbles" is her famous nickname. No points unless you named both.

32. Estelle Liebling.

33. Among them are Sarah Caldwell, the Boston Opera Company; Carol Fox, the Chicago Lyric Opera; Mary Garden, the Chicago Opera; Emma Carelli, the Rome Opera; Rosa Ponselle, the Baltimore Civic Opera; and Kirsten Flagstad, the Oslo Opera.

34. *Uncle Sol Solves It.*

35. "Major Bowes' Capitol Family Hour," "Our Gal Sunday," "The Cresta Blanca Carnival."

36. The Queen of the Night, Queen Elizabeth, the Queen of Shemakha in Rimski-Korsakov's *Golden Cockerel*, Anna Bolena, Juana in *La Loca*, Cleopatra and Mary Stewart.

37. The Philadelphia Grand Opera Company in 1947.

38. Violetta in *La Traviata*.

39. Rosalinda in *Die Fledermaus*.

Scene Five: A Galaxy of Stars

40. It was her response to impresario Colonel Mapleson's offer of only half her salary in advance. The canny Patti knew that only by refusing to sing could she collect her entire salary from the perennially broke Mapleson.

41. James McCracken, now one of our great Otellos, made his debut as Melot, but was first noted as the Messenger in *Aida*. Irving Kolodin writes in his book *The Metropolitan Opera* that newcomer Giorgio Tozzi marveled, "If they have that kind of voice for the Messenger, what must the leading tenor sound like?"

42. Francesca Caccini (1587–c. 1640), daughter of Giulio Caccini (1545–1618). She sang the florid roles composed for her by her father, establishing nepotism as a prima donna's tool at a very early stage in opera history.

43. Caruso! His teacher Vergine, who is only remembered for his inaccurate predictions about Caruso, also said this about the tenor's voice: "It is like gold at the bottom of the Tiber, hardly worth digging for."

44. (a) Adelina Patti   (e) Evelyn Lear
     (b) Lilli Lehmann   (f) Giuseppe Danise
     (c) Mario   (g) Elisabeth Rethberg
     (d) Christa Ludwig   (h) James McCracken

45. Marian Anderson first sang her only role at the Met, Ulrica in *Un Ballo in Maschera*, on January 5, 1955.

46. To circumvent the Papal Ban against women on the stage, the *castrati* at first sang only women's parts, but composers began to make use of their remarkable talents for heroic male roles. For amusing anecdotes about *castrati* and how easily they could pass as women, one should read Jacques Casanova's spicy memoirs, in which the great lover confesses how he was taken in by a *castrato* posing as a woman.

47. Francesca Cuzzoni and Faustina Bordoni were the first in that tradition. Managers tried to take advantage of the publicity of their rivalry by starring them together, but the results were unfortunate. When Bononcini's *Astianatte* featured the two divas in London in 1727, the evening ended in a hair-pulling brawl onstage. A similar production of Handel's *Alessandro* ended in the same manner, and it was concluded that it was safer not to pair them onstage.

Later rivalries included Maria Malibran vs. Henriette Sontag, Adelina Patti vs. Etelka Gerster and Nellie Melba vs. Lillian Nordica. Lilli Lehmann also feuded with Nordica, once informing her, "I am not taking any pupils this season." Most recently, the fans of Maria Callas and Renata Tebaldi have kept the tradition alive.

48. Enrico Caruso and Geraldine Farrar made this famous recording, on which Farrar's ad-lib can still clearly be heard.

49. Louis XIV, the "Sun King" of France, performed as a dancer in opera-ballets by Lully.

50. She sang 170 different roles.

51. (a) Teresa Carreño.
    (b) Amelita Galli-Curci.
    (c) Judith Blegen.
    (d) Marcella Sembrich delighted the audience at a benefit for Henry Abbey in 1884, when she played the De Beriot violin concerto and a Chopin mazurka on the piano before singing "Ah, non giunge" from *La Sonnambula*.

52. Unlike Caruso, who was only comfortable up to B flat, Hippolito Lazaro was celebrated for his high notes. A fierce rival, who had to placate Caruso in order to sing at the Met, Lazaro nevertheless remained in the shadow of Caruso's great fame, proving that high notes aren't everything.

53. The ones most often on menus are: Spaghetti Caruso, named for Enrico Caruso; Chicken Tetrazzini, named for the soprano Luisa Tetrazzini (no plucked chicken she!); and Pêche Melba, named for coloratura soprano Nellie Melba, who wasn't exactly peaches and cream!

54. Contralto Marietta Alboni was as wonderful a singer as she was huge. Rossini coined this description.

55. (a) Richard Strauss   (e) Richard Bonynge
     (b) Felix Weingartner   (f) Frieder Weissmann
     (c) Anton Seidl   (g) André Kostelanetz
     (d) Henry Lewis

56. "One god, one Farinelli!" was the cry of an enthusiastic fan. Perhaps the greatest singer of all time, Carlo Broschi, known as Farinelli, is popularly credited with curing the madness of Philip V of Spain by singing the same four songs to him every night for ten years at 50,000 francs a year, which isn't bad retirement pay!

57. Pasquale Brignoli was the first star tenor in America. Italo Campanini succeeded him.

58. Jenny Lind.

59. Christine Nilsson and Sigrid Arnoldson were also called Swedish Nightingales.

60. Leo Slezak ad-libbed it when the swan boat that takes Lohengrin away in the last act mistakenly left him onstage.

61. (a) Gabrielle Krauss
     (b) Marie Wilt
     (c) Christine Nilsson
     (d) Leontyne Price

62. Melba, a name Ponselle took in honor of her heroine, Nellie Melba.

63. Maria Malibran.

64. (a) Josef Rosenblatt, called the Jewish Caruso.
(b) Hermann Jadlowker, tenor from Riga, Latvia, whom Richard Strauss called "my favorite tenor;" and Richard Tucker.

65. Adelina Patti never sang *Norma* herself, although her career started at the age of seven, when she sang "Casta Diva" perched on top of a table.

66. The four singers who premiered Bellini's *I Puritani* became known as the *Puritani* Quartet. They were Giulia Grisi, soprano; Giovanni Battista Rubini, tenor; Antonio Tamburini, bass; and Luigi Lablache, bass. Three of these singers, Grisi, Tamburini and Lablache, later created Donizetti's *Don Pasquale,* while the tenor role was taken by Giovanni Mario, the husband of Grisi.

67. Madame Charles Cahier, born in Nashville, Tennessee.

68. Caruso is said to be the man who made the gramophone, but his immediate predecessor at the Met, Jean de Reszke, declined to record. There are rumors of test pressings lying in a Paris bank vault, but the only clue to his artistry (considered by contemporary critics superior to that of Caruso) comes from Mapleson cylinders made live at the Met in 1901.

69. Gilbert Duprez in Rossini's *William Tell.* Rossini was not amused and later told Duprez to "leave your high C in the vestibule when you visit me."

70. Marie Cornélie Falcon's career lasted from 1832 to 1838, but made such an impression that all subsequent French dramatic sopranos are classified as "falcons."

71. This was Charlotte Cushman (1816–1876), who first made her name as an opera singer, although she is now remembered for her achievements as America's first great actress.

72. (a) Fort Worth, Texas, 1962;
(b) *Lucia di Lammermoor;*
(c) Lily Pons.

73. Nellie Melba, Sigrid Arnoldson, Bessie Abott, Suzanne Adams, Emma Eames, Frances Alda, Emma Calvé, Blanche Marchesi, Sybil Sanderson, Ilma di Murska. There are many more, so if you came up with six of the above caliber, take the points.

74. Jenny Lind. John Genin recouped far more than the price of his ticket by selling hats because of the publicity he received.

75. Chief Caupolican, a Chilean-born Indian who, although he was no Ruffo, did find success on Broadway playing the chief in *Whoopee!*

76. Adelina Patti, at 5 feet 2 inches.

77. Geraldine Farrar, at the curtain of Humperdinck's *Die Königskinder*.

78. By the winds of fate, Lillian Nordica was saved the trouble of divorcing her first husband, Frederick Gower.

79. Marie Van Zandt, the creator of Lakmé, was born in New York City in 1861. An extraordinary singer, today mostly forgotten, she was once praised for "her unusual type, charming and untamed; her presence at once chaste and provocative, less voluptuous than the Rarahu of Loti, but designed to awaken the same sensations, her childlike graces, her physique, in a word, designated her as the living personification of Lakmé. . . . in future the part could never be played under a different guise."

80. Rosa Raisa, in Chicago, because a zealous stagehand had overcushioned the pot with elastic material. Her bounce was visible from the auditorium.

81. Minnie Hauk, in 1878.

82. Gertrud Wettergren recorded this dubious achievement in 1936 as a last-minute replacement for Rosa Ponselle.

83. In Chicago in 1937.

84. Niccolò Tacchinardi, whose great beauty of voice and style so overcame the effect of his physical appearance that he was acclaimed for his portrayal of Don Giovanni. His daughter was Fanny Tacchinardi Persiani, for whom Donizetti wrote *Lucia di Lammermoor*.

85. Tenor Adolphe Nourrit, whose career ended when he committed suicide in despair over the successes of his rival, Duprez.

86. (a) Sophie Arnould (1740–1802). *Arnoldiana*, published in 1813, contains her witty sayings.
(b) Emmy Destinn.
(c) Helen Traubel wrote *The Metropolitan Opera Murders*.

87. Soprano Emma Eames (1865–1952) was the daughter of American missionaries.

88. Rubini "patented" the Rubini Sob, although so many

tenors have since used it that it is, alas, now in the public domain.

89. Kiri Te Kanawa.

90. Figaro was his favorite role, Don Giovanni his least favorite, because the Don never got the girl!

91. "Some Enchanted Evening."

92. Henriette Sontag died of cholera in Mexico, and Lillian Nordica was shipwrecked off Java.

93. Lilli Lehmann played Carlo Broschi (Farinelli) in Auber's *La Part du Diable*.

94. Titta Ruffo was named after his father's dog, Ruffo!

95. Victor Herbert.

96. (a) Maude Fay, (b) Leon Rains, (c) Putnam Griswold.

97. (a) Clara Louise Kellogg, (b) Mario Chamlee, (c) Marian Telva.

98. Jan Peerce, who kindly sent us this question.

99. (a) Maria Callas.
  (b) Lillian Nordica. Her real name was Lillian Norton.
  (c) Florence Macbeth, born in Minnesota in 1891, was for years the leading soprano of the Chicago Opera.
  (d) Emma Nevada (1859–1940) took her name from nearby Nevada City, California.

Score: _____

INTERIOR VIEW OF NIBLO'S THEATRE, NEW YORK.

THE NEW GRAND OPERA-HOUSE AT PARIS.—[See Page 583.]

ACT II

Opera Houses and Cities

Scene One: Metropolitan Opera Trivia

Answers on p. 42.

100. Why was the Metropolitan Opera House built? (8)

101. What opera opened the Met in 1883? (2)

102. Name the tenor, baritone, bass and mezzo who starred in that opening-night cast in 1883. (1 point for each, for a total of 4)

103. On the night the Met opened in 1883, the cream of New York gentry was at the old, established Academy of Music, also opening for the season on the same night.
(a) What opera was performed at the Academy?
(b) What prima donna was the featured star?
   (2 points for each, for a total of 4)

104. What was the nickname of the old Met? (1)

105. Who were the two architects of the old Met? (3)

106. Who was the architect of the new Met at Lincoln Center? (1)

107. In the 1930s plans were discussed for a new Met. Who was the architect who drew up the plans? HINT: He was a famous stage designer for the Ziegfeld Follies as well as the Met. (2)

108. Since its first season in 1883, the Metropolitan Opera has been dark for only one full season. What season and why? (2)

109. When were the first live recordings of a Met performance made? (1)

Met Managers

110. Possibly even harder than being president of the United States or even mayor of New York is the job of general manager of the Metropolitan Opera. What president or mayor has had to deal with prima donnas, temperamental tenors or, worse, their families?
(a) How many managers has the Met had? (2)
(b) Name all of them for 10 points. (10)
(c) Which were singers? (3)
(d) Which were conductors? (1)
(e) Which died before their first seasons? (3)
(f) Who was the watchdog co-manager that Farrar and Caruso almost quit over? (2)
(g) Who was the first American manager? (4)
   (25 total)

111. What composers' names were enshrined over the old Met's proscenium? (3)

112. What famous couturier provided the entire wardrobe, "every costume, every shoe and stocking," for the Met's very first season in 1883? (3)

113. What marriage caused the groom to be taken out of consideration for the job of manager of the Met? (5)

114. When Toscanini first came to the Met in 1908, what preeminent conductor was already there? (1)

115. Who sang Otello for the first time during a Metropolitan Opera season? (2)

116. Before Joan Sutherland sang it in 1970, only four sopranos had sung Norma at the Metropolitan. Name them in order. (4)

117. What was Kirsten Flagstad's debut role at the Met? (2)

118. Before Set Svanholm, only one other tenor at the Metropolitan had sung both Tristan and Radames in one season. Who was he? (1)

119. Who were the only father and son to conduct at the Met? (2)

120. On the same day Marion Talley made her highly publicized debut in 1926, one of the truly great singers of the century debuted during the matinee. Name the singer. (3)

121. What famous singer left the Met during the Depression as the only member of the roster to refuse a salary cut? (1)

122. What music festival was founded by Sir Rudolf Bing? (2)

123. What famous singer refused to sing at the Met because of a dread of sea voyages? (3)

124. Who was the first singer to serve on the board of directors of the Metropolitan Opera? (1)

125. What singer used to joke about listing Sir Rudolf Bing as a dependent on her tax returns? (1)

126. In what language was *Carmen* first presented at the Met? (2)

127. Toscanini conducted a celebrated revival of *Carmen* at the Met. For 2 points each, name the Carmen and the Micaëla at the first *Carmen* Toscanini conducted there. (4)

128. Who has the distinction of being the first soprano to sing a barefoot Amina in *La Sonnambula* at the Met? (8)

129. What role did Geraldine Farrar sing at her farewell Met performance? (2)

130. What is the only Puccini opera the Met has *not* staged as of 1981? (3)

131. From the time of his debut in 1903, Caruso sang at every opening during his reign at the Met, except for one when he allowed another singer to debut as the undisputed star of the evening. For two points each, name the singer and the opera. (4)

132. What was Marilyn Horne's debut role at the Met? (1)

133. What opera did James Levine first conduct at the Met? (2)

134. What opera opened both Sir Rudolf Bing's first and last Met seasons? (2)

135. What was the last song to be heard in the old Met? (2)

136. What three operas opened the ill-fated "Mini-Met"? (9)

137. Where was the "Mini-Met"? (1)

138. In what role did Kiri Te Kanawa debut at the Met? (1)

139. What was the first nineteenth-century grand opera presented at the Met at Lincoln Center? (7)

140. What was the first American opera presented at the Metropolitan? (5)

141. What two Met baritones rose to stardom via the relatively minor role of Ford in Verdi's *Falstaff?* (3)

142. Who was the first winner of the Metropolitan Opera Auditions of the Air? (5)

143. What Met conductor composed recitatives for *Fidelio?* (3)

144. What do the two groups of composers listed below have to do with the Met? (6)
Group One: Franco Vittadini; Alberto Franchetti; Richard Hageman; Primo Riccitelli; Ernest II, Duke of Saxe-Coburg-Gotha; Raoul Laparra; John Seymour; Marvin David Levy; Felice Lattuada; Karel Weis; Xavier Leroux.
Group Two: George Frideric Handel; Franz Joseph Haydn; Jean-Baptiste Lully; Jean-Philippe Rameau; Luigi Cherubini; George Gershwin.

145. Name two instrumentalists from the Met Opera orchestra who went on to bigger things. (2 points for each, for a total of 4)

146. Name the famous Valentine in Gounod's *Faust* who designed sets for a different Gounod opera at the Met. (4)

147. Conductors Leopold Stokowski and Eugene Ormandy, maestri of the Philadelphia Orchestra, each conducted one opera at the Metropolitan. What were the two operas? (3)

Scene Two: Opera in America

148. When and with what opera did the New York City Opera make its premiere? (5) Who was the star? (2)

149. What opera did the New York City Opera first present at the New York State Theater at Lincoln Center? (8)

150. Who was the architect of the New York State Theater, the home of the New York City Opera? (1)

151. What was the City Center, the first home of the New York City Opera, before it became a theater? (1)

152. What was the first opera house built in the United States? (8)

153. Where was the first opera presented in the United States? (5)

154. (a) Where was the first Italian opera, performed in Italian, presented in the United States?
(b) What was the opera?
(c) What troupe gave it?
(d) Name the leading tenor and soprano.
(2 points for each part for a total of 8)

155. What American opera house presented the American

premieres of Berlioz's *Benvenuto Cellini*, Gounod's *The Queen of Sheba*, Lalo's *Le Roi d'Ys*, Massenet's *Hérodiade* and Saint-Saëns's *Samson et Dalila?* (4)

156. What was the first performance of an Italian opera in America? Who was the composer? (8)

157. What was the name of the important American house opened in 1859? (6)

158. In the nineteenth century four major opera houses were built in New York. Name them in order for 10 points. (10)

159. What opera company gave the American premieres of Strauss's *Die Frau Ohne Schatten* and Poulenc's *The Dialogues of the Carmelites?* (3)

160. Where did Birgit Nilsson make her American debut? (3)

161. Opera managers are fired all the time. However, one sued for damages and won. Who was he? (2)

162. What is the most important opera to have its United States premiere in Brooklyn? (3)

163. What was the first home of the San Francisco Opera? (6)

164. What was the second home of the San Francisco Opera? (9)

165. What opera opened the first season of the San Francisco Opera in 1923? (3)

166. What opera and what diva were featured for the

opening of the San Francisco War Memorial, the current home of the San Francisco Opera, in 1932? (3)

167. Who was the founder and first director of the San Francisco Opera? (2)

168. Name the five major opera companies that have performed as resident companies in Chicago. (10)

169. Name the popular nineteenth-century opera that was the first grand opera to be performed in both Chicago and San Francisco. (6)

170. What operatic masterpiece had its American premiere at Wellesley College in Massachusetts in 1938? (6)

171. Name the five directors of the New York City Opera. (1 point for each, for a total of 5)

Scene Three: The International World of Opera

172. Where was the first opera house opened for business? (4)

173. Who was the architect of La Scala? (9)

174. What opera opened La Scala in 1778? (10)

175. What was the principal opera house in Milan before La Scala was built? (6)

176. During Allied bombing in World War II, La Scala was gutted. It continued, however, to give performances at another theater until 1946. What was the name of that theater? (5)

THE BROOKLYN ACADEMY OF MUSIC.—EXTERIOR.—[See Page 78.]

THE BROOKLYN ACADEMY OF MUSIC.—INTERIOR. OPENING CONCERT ON TUESDAY, JANUARY 15, 1861.—[See Page 78.]

177. What was the first Mozart opera staged at La Scala? (5)

178. Name five (out of six) operas Donizetti wrote for La Scala. (6 points each, for a total of 30)

179. What was the first opera presented at Covent Garden? (4)

180. How many Covent Garden theaters have there been? (4)

181. What opera house was located at a goose market? (3)

182. Name two opera houses built on the site of a convent. (3)

183. What city has seen the most world premieres of operas? (1)

184. What caused:
    (a) the greatest opera riot in Paris?
    (b) the greatest opera riot in London?
(2 points each, for a total of 4)

SUNDAY AMUSEMENTS IN NEW ORLEANS—A CREOLE NIGHT AT THE FRENCH OPERA-HOUSE.—Sketched by our Special Artist, A. R. Waud.—[See First Page.]

SUNDAY AMUSEMENTS IN NEW ORLEANS—THE COCKPIT.—Sketched by our Special Artist, A. R. Waud.—[See First Page.]

ACT II: Answers

Scene One: Metropolitan Opera Trivia

100. The Metropolitan Opera House was built so the new rich of New York could have opera boxes of their own. Lilli Lehmann explained in her massive autobiography *My Path Through Life*:

As, on a particular evening, one of the millionairesses did not receive the box in which she intended to shine because another woman had anticipated her, the husband of the former took prompt action and caused the Metropolitan Opera House to rise.

101. *Faust*, by Charles Gounod.

102. Italo Campanini, Giuseppe del Puente, Franco Novara and Sofia Scalchi.

103. (a) Bellini's *La Sonnambula*.
(b) Etelka Gerster.

104. The Yellow Brick Brewery, derisively named by Colonel Mapleson.

105. Josiah Cleaveland Cady and Louis de Coppet Bergh designed the old Met. They were also the designers of the American Museum of Natural History, which had a better fate.

106. Wallace K. Harrison.

107. Joseph Urban.

108. 1892–93, due to a fire which nearly ended the Met for good.

109. In 1901 Lionel Mapleson made recordings of live performances from the wings with a primitive cylinder machine given to him by Thomas Edison. Despite their often horrendous sound, these recordings provide a precious glimpse of a truly golden age and are the only clues we have to the voices of Jean de Reszke, Milka Ternina and Fritzi Scheff.

110. (a) Thirteen.
  (b) Henry E. Abbey, Leopold Damrosch, Edmund Stanton, John B. Schoeffel, Maurice Grau, Heinrich Conried, Giulio Gatti-Casazza, Herbert Witherspoon, Edward Johnson, Rudolf Bing, Goeran Gentele, Schuyler Chapin, Anthony Bliss.
  (c) Herbert Witherspoon and Edward Johnson.
  (d) Leopold Damrosch.
  (e) Herbert Witherspoon and Goeran Gentele died before their first seasons.
  (f) Andreas Dippel was the singer appointed as co-manager with Gatti-Casazza in order to prevent him from making the Met too "Italianate." When Dippel was fired after a trial period, Geraldine Farrar instigated a petition signed by herself, Caruso, Scotti, Eames and Sembrich demanding Gatti's "same privileges" be given to Dippel. The singers were told to shut up and sing. Eames and Sembrich retired, Caruso and Scotti pointed to Farrar as the troublemaker, and Farrar decided that if you can't lick them, join them, and she became friendly to the new management, especially Toscanini (the unofficial music director).
  (g) Henry E. Abbey, the first manager!

111. The names of Mozart, Gluck, Gounod, Verdi,

Beethoven and Wagner appeared in bold letters over the old Met's proscenium.

112. Worth of Paris, in those days the most glamorous name in couture. The Met lost $600,000 in this first season.

113. The marriage of Covent Garden impresario Ernest Gye to soprano Emma Albani, a rival of Met favorite Christine Nilsson, cost him the post, as loyal fans of Nilsson did not want to see her slighted for Albani. Ironically, a later manager, Giulio Gatti-Casazza, married soprano Frances Alda, causing Geraldine Farrar to complain of consideration given to, in Farrar's opinion, "a second-rate soprano."

114. Gustav Mahler announced that he welcomed working with a conductor of the caliber of Toscanini, but he quickly grew disenchanted with being number two, or, as Irving Kolodin wrote in his book *The Metropolitan Opera,* "supplementing the efforts of Toscanini." Mahler soon withdrew to run the New York Philharmonic.

115. Jean de Reszke, in what was probably his least effective portrayal. The opera's creator, Francesco Tamagno, had sung the title role at the opera house two years earlier, but after a regular season, so it doesn't count!

116. Lilli Lehmann, Rosa Ponselle, Gina Cigna, Zinka Milanov.

117. Sieglinde.

118. Jean de Reszke.

119. Leopold and Walter Damrosch.

120. Lauritz Melchior. He recalled hearing the hammering backstage as Marion Talley's father installed a telegraph to wire home the "good news."

121. Beniamino Gigli.

122. The Edinburgh International Festival of Music and Drama in Scotland. Earlier, Bing had helped John Christie organize the festival founded at Glyndebourne.

123. Mattia Battistini (1856–1928), the undisputed "king of baritones," had once journeyed to South America, and he swore never to cross the ocean again.

124. Lucrezia Bori.

125. Birgit Nilsson.

126. In Italian. Interestingly, it was given in Italian at its first New York performance at the Academy of Music in 1878.

127. Maria Gay was the Carmen, Geraldine Farrar the Micaëla. (If you said Farrar was the Carmen, you do not get any points, although she did sing the role with Toscanini much later.)

128. Elvira de Hidalgo, in 1910. She is remembered more as the teacher of Maria Callas than for this distinction.

129. Zazà.

130. *Edgar*.

131. Geraldine Farrar, who made her debut in *Roméo et Juliette* on November 26, 1906.

132. Adalgisa in *Norma,* March 3, 1970.

133. Puccini's *Tosca*, in 1971.

134. Verdi's *Don Carlo*, first in 1950 and finally in 1971.

135. "Auld Lang Syne," on April 17, 1966.

136. *Syllabaire pour Phèdre* by Ohana, *Dido and Aeneas* by Purcell and *Four Saints in Three Acts* by Thomson, in 1973.

137. The Forum Auditorium in the Metropolitan Opera House at Lincoln Center. This tiny auditorium is where the "Met Opera Quiz" radio broadcast originates. It was hopelessly tiny for even the most intimate opera.

138. Desdemona in 1974.

139. Ponchielli's *La Giocanda*, the first performance after the opening night fiasco, *Antony and Cleopatra*, in 1966.

140. *The Pipe of Desire*, by Frederick Converse, on March 18, 1910, with an all-American cast, shared the bill with *Pagliacci*.

141. Lawrence Tibbett and Giuseppe Campanari.

142. Thomas L. Thomas, in 1936.

143. Artur Bodanzky.

144. The first group is the motley collection of composers who have had at least one opera presented at the Met. Not one of the second group, all undisputed masters, has had even one opera presented at the Met.

145. Victor Herbert, the operetta composer, and Giuseppe Campanari, the celebrated baritone, both began as cellists with the Met Orchestra.

146. French baritone Victor Maurel, for the production of *Mireille* in 1919.

147. Ormandy conducted *Die Fledermaus*, and Stokowski, *Turandot*.

Scene Two: Opera in America

148. Formed to offer quality performances of opera at affordable prices, the New York City Opera debuted on February 21, 1944, with *Tosca* under the directorship of László Hálász. The star was Dusolina Giannini.

149. Ginastera's *Don Rodrigo,* on February 22, 1966. At least the New York City Opera's selection did not fare any more poorly than the Met's Lincoln Center opener.

150. Philip Johnson.

151. A Masonic temple.

152. The Théâtre du Spectacle in New Orleans, built in 1792.

153. Charleston, South Carolina, in 1735. This was *Flora*, an English ballad opera presented in a courtroom.

154. (a) In 1825, at the Park Theatre in New York.
  (b), (c) and (d) Manuel Garcia, star of the Garcia Troupe, sang the role of Almaviva, a role he had created, in *Il Barbiere di Siviglia*. His soprano was his daughter, Maria, later Malibran.

155. The French Opera House in New Orleans.

156. *The Barber of Seville* by Giovanni Paisiello was presented in English in Baltimore in 1794.

157. The French Opera House in New Orleans.

158. The Italian Opera House, the Astor Place Opera, the Academy of Music, the Metropolitan Opera House.

159. The San Francisco Opera.

160. The San Francisco Opera.

161. László Hálász, the first director of the New York City Opera. Content with collecting the money, he did not return.

162. Mozart's *The Abduction from the Seraglio,* presented by the Brooklyn Operatic Circle as *Belmonte e Constanze* in 1860. (Give yourself the points if you came up with another Brooklyn premiere arguably as important as this one.)

163. The Civic Auditorium.

164. Dreamland Auditorium, from 1928 to 1930.

165. *La Bohème*.

166. *Tosca,* starring Claudia Muzio.

167. Gaetano Merola.

168. The Chicago-Philadelphia Opera, the Chicago Opera Association, the Chicago Civic Opera Company, the Ravinia Festival, the Chicago Lyric Opera.

169. *La Sonnambula*.

GRAND FANCY-DRESS BALL AT THE OPENING OF THE NEW ACADEMY OF MUSIC.—[See Page 166.]

170. Gluck's *Alceste*.

171. László Hálász, Joseph Rosenstock, Erich Leinsdorf, Julius Rudel, Beverly Sills.

Scene Three: The International World of Opera

172. Venice, in 1637, the San Cassiano.

173. Giuseppe Piermarini.

174. *Europa riconosciuta* by Salieri.

175. Teatro Ducale.

176. Teatro Lirico.

177. *Così fan Tutte* in 1807.

178. *Chiara e Serafina; Ugo, Conte di Parigi; Lucrezia Borgia; Gemma di Vergy; Maria Padilla; Gianni di Parigi.*

179. *The Beggar's Opera*.

180. Three.

181. The Hamburg Opera, founded in 1678.

182. The Munich Opera, built in 1818, has seen the premieres of some very unconventlike operas, including *Tristan und Isolde*. Covent Garden, of course, is located on the site of a convent garden.

183. Paris.

184. (a) The notorious Jockey Club Riot was caused when

Wagner inserted the required ballet into *Tann-häuser*'s first act rather than the standard second act. So the premiere of the Paris version of *Tannhäuser* became a fiasco when the dandies of the Jockey Club arrived fashionably late after their leisurely meal, to find that they had missed the ballet. They rioted, and Wagner had to flee for his life!

(b) The London impresario Laporte tried to break the power of his stars by not reengaging the bass, Antonio Tamburini. On the first night Tamburini would have sung, the audience rebelled. Only an announcement that the bass would be reengaged ended the infamous Tamburini Riot.

Score: _____

SIGNOR GIUSEPPE VERDI.

ACT III

The Composers and Their Operas

In this section the opera's the thing, and you'll have to know more than simply who's singing tonight.

Answers on page 77.

Scene One: Beginner's Luck, the Dawn of Opera

185. What is considered the first opera ever composed? Name the composer. (4 points for each, for a total of 8)

186. Who was the most dominant force in opera during the eighteenth century? (2)

187. Who sang Belinda to Kirsten Flagstad's Dido in the historic revival of Purcell's *Dido and Aeneas* at the Mermaid Theatre, during the 1951 Festival of Britain? (3)

188. The marriage of King Louis XIV of France to Marie Thérèse of Spain was celebrated with an opera performance.
(a) What opera was specifically composed to celebrate the wedding? (3)
(b) Who wrote the ballet music for it? (2)

(c) What opera was performed? (5)
(Total for this question is 10)

189. Louis XIV of France was a great opera fan. He was especially fond of one opera, which he exclaimed he "could hear every day." Name the opera. (6)

190. What are the three celebrated opera-composer rivalries of the eighteenth century? (Take 10 points if you can name *all* three.)

191. What "war" was started by a performance of *La Serva Padrona* in Paris in 1752? (4)

192. Some think anyone would have to be crazy to compose an opera, but very brilliant people have tried their hands at it.
(a) Name a famous philosopher who composed a celebrated opera. (2)
(b) Name a great chess master who was a successful opera composer. (2)
    (4 points total)

193. Most opera lovers are aware of the great "reform" operas of Christoph Willibald von Gluck, beginning with his immortal *Orfeo ed Euridice*. Can you name the librettist for *Orfeo* and most of his other reform operas? (3)

194. Who wrote and composed the original *The Beggar's Opera*? (3)

195. The Largo from *Serse*, "Ombra mai fù," is probably the most famous aria Handel ever composed and has been sung in modern times by sopranos, basses, baritones and tenors alike. Despite the interest today in "historical accuracy" in performances, however, it is very unlikely that we can hear the Largo sung as it was originally. Not unless we bring the surgeons back into the opera world. Who was the singer who gave the first performance of the Largo? (5)

196. What opera did Handel compose in two weeks for his first production in England in 1711? (8)

197. Which Haydn opera had to wait 150 years for its first performance? (3)

198. Who was composer Salieri's most famous pupil? (1)

Scene Two: Mozart

199. At what age did Mozart compose his first opera, *La Finta Semplice?* (3)

200. In *Don Giovanni*, for one broken-hearted victim, Leporello lists the Don's conquests: "Madamina! il catalogo è questo."
(a) According to Leporello, how many women has the Don seduced? (4)
(b) Who is the lady to whom Leporello obligingly relates all of this? (1)

201. At the time Lorenzo Da Ponte was writing his masterful libretto for *Don Giovanni,* he was simultaneously working on two others, *Assur* and *L'Abore di Diana,* for two of Mozart's rivals. Who were their composers? (7)

202. It seems strange to us today, but there was quite a lot of criticism when Ezio Pinza was given the role of Don Giovanni, as at the time it was traditional for a baritone to sing it. Of course Pinza was so brilliant that he established a new tradition, carried on by basses like Cesare Siepi. Would the critics have complained about Pinza if they had known that in the nineteenth century it was also traditional for the role to be sung by a tenor? Name three famous tenors to sing Don Giovanni. (5)

203. What are the two immortal operas which were created at the behest of Emanuel Schikaneder? (3)

204. What famous lover gave advice to Mozart and Da Ponte on the creation of *Don Giovanni?* (1)

205. Which of Mozart's operas was based on a true story? (2)

206. What famous composer was the first English Papageno? (9)

207. What was the literary source of the "Egyptian" parts of *Die Zauberflöte?* (9)

208. What is the only completely original libretto, i.e., not taken from another play or libretto, written for Mozart by Lorenzo Da Ponte? (1)

209. What was the only role Adelina Patti would sing in *Don Giovanni?* (1)

210. *Bluebeard* and "Im Tiefen Keller" were the successful compositions of two of the singers who participated in the world premieres of Mozart operas. Take 5 points for each singer if you can name the singer *and* the opera he sang in at its premiere. (10 points total)

211. What is the opera Mozart wrote based on the story called *Lulu?* (5)

212. Whom does Figaro marry? (1)

213. A composer named Wenzel Müller wrote an opera

with a story very similar to that of *Die Zauberflöte* in 1791. However, the hero used a different "magic" instrument. What was it? (9)

214. What is Figaro's real name? (1)

215. What Mozart libretto did one Carl Ludwig Giesecke claim to have written? (5)

216. The operatic masterpieces *The Barber of Seville* and *The Marriage of Figaro* are based on the first two plays in a Figaro trilogy by Caron de Beaumarchais. Darius Milhaud composed an opera based on the third play of the series, but as he was no Mozart or Rossini, it is not very well known. Can you name the third play? (8)

217. The plot of *The Marriage of Figaro* hinges upon Count Almaviva's attempt to revive a lascivious feudal privilege he had abolished to celebrate his marriage to Rosina. What was this privilege called and what did it entail? (4)

218. What three operas did Mozart quote in *Don Giovanni?* Name them and their composers. (7)

219. Who was the music teacher of Mozart's son? (2)

220. What was the name of the unfinished opera from which Mozart lifted music for *The Abduction from the Seraglio?* (4)

221. Who was the woman who refused Mozart's hand in marriage? (3)

222. What Metropolitan revival of a Mozart opera was so excoriated by the critics but drew an avalanche of support and letters of protest to the critics? (4)

223. How did Bruno Walter's cook influence the selection of a Don Giovanni for the Salzburg Festival? (5)

Scene Three: Bel Canto Mad Scenes

224. What composer advised Bellini in his work on *I Puritani?* (2)

225. What Donizetti opera has three leading roles for tenor? (2)

226. Rossini was contracted by Duke Cesarini, manager of the Argentine Theater in Rome, to compose two operas. One was *Torvaldo e Dorliska*, a flop. What was the other? (2)

227. Name all the participants in the famous sextette in *Lucia di Lammermoor*. (We'll accept just the first names.) (6)

228. When Donizetti, who wrote the last act of *La Favorite* in three hours, was informed that a rival had written a masterpiece in thirteen days, he replied, "Why not? He's so lazy!" Who was the "lazy" composer and what was the opera? (3)

229. Many of Gaetano Donizetti's operas feature mad scenes. These are the scenes that give the soprano, and sometimes the baritone or tenor, opportunities for crazy flights of coloratura. Can you name seven Donizetti operas with mad scenes? (5)

230. The amazing Barber of Seville has all the following resources except for which two? (3)
(a) a guitar
(b) a razor
(c) a shaving mug and cream
(d) a barbershop
(e) a barber pole

231. Queen Maria Cristina of the Two Sicilies was so impressed by the dress rehearsal of a Donizetti opera in 1834 that she fainted! What was this moving opera? (4)

232. Bel Canto composer Bellini died tragically young and composed a pitifully small number of operas, so you should know them all.
(a) Can you name the student opera of Bellini's that so impressed the impresario Barbaja? (4)
(b) What opera did Barbaja commission from Bellini after the student performance? (3)

233. At the conclusion of a performance of Edgardo's last aria in *Lucia*, such a commotion arose that the lobby policeman rushed in, thinking there was a riot. It was just the audience cheering for an encore! Who was the tenor who created this excitement? (2)

234. Who was the tenor who claimed to have helped Donizetti compose the last scene of *Lucia di Lammermoor?* (3)

235. In Alexandre Dumas's masterpiece, *The Count of Monte Cristo*, a Donizetti opera is performed in Rome. What is the opera? (5)

Scene Four: Verdi

236. Who wrote libretti for Verdi, after having earlier publicly criticized the composer? (4)

Learning at the Master's Feet

237. (a) What later famous conductor volunteered to play cello in the first performance of *Otello?* (1)
(b) What later famous conductor played the glockenspiel for another conductor's 1937 perform-

ances of *The Magic Flute* in Salzburg? (3)

(c) Who was the conductor of *The Magic Flute* performances in Salzburg in 1937? (2)

238. Where did the world premiere of *Aida* take place? (1)

239. Who was the conductor of the world premiere of *Aida*, and how was he most famous? (4)

240. Who was the librettist of *Aida*? (2)

241. Who was the librettist of *Rigoletto*? (3)

242. What was the name of the Victor Hugo play that was adapted for *Rigoletto*? (6)

243. What did the Italians really mean when they cried "Viva Verdi!" (4)

Scene Five: Puccini and the Other "Verists"

244. Name two Met Toscas who decided to be blond rather than the specified "Bruna Floria." (3)

245. What opera by Puccini is based on what work by Dante? (3)

246. Who was the first Tosca to sing "Vissi d'arte" in a prone position? (2)

247. How did Puccini earn the money to buy an American motorboat? (6)

248. What are the four Puccini operas to receive their world premieres at the Met? (2)

249. Puccini always had a special feeling for his heroines, and he was very particular in choosing the sopranos who would create them in the premieres of his operas.

(a) Who was the only soprano to create more than one heroine in world premieres of Puccini operas? (3)

(b) What were the roles? (2)

(c) Who was the first Madame Butterfly? (2)

(d) Who created Madame Butterfly in the premiere of the revised version? (4)

(e) Who created Suor Angelica? (3)

(f) What role did the soprano Hariclea Darclée create? (2)

250. What connection did Puccini have with the ballet *Giselle*? (1)

251. (a) Who was the author of the stage versions of *Madame Butterfly* and *The Girl of the Golden West*? (2)

(b) Who originally portrayed these roles in their first dramatic performances? (3)

Tosca

252. (a) Who is the original author of the play *Tosca*? (1)

(b) What famous actor claimed to have come up with the idea first, in a scenario entitled *Nadjezda*? (4)

(c) Who first portrayed Tosca in the play? (1)

253. Name the librettists of Puccini's *La Bohème*. (2)

254. What Puccini opera was initially a failure? (1)

255. Puccini was only one of many composers to set Carlo Gozzi's 1762 play, *Turandot*, to music. Name another famous composer whose *Turandot* premiered in 1917. (3)

Puccini's Opera Quiz

256. In *Turandot* Calaf is asked three riddles. He then asks Turandot a question. In the opera only three out of the four are answered correctly. Can you do better?
Turandot's questions:
(a) What is born every night and dies every day?
(b) What is sometimes like a fever but goes cold when you die, that fires up when you think of great deeds?
(c) What is the ice that sets you on fire?
Calaf answers them correctly, and then has one for Turandot:
(d) What does Calaf ask Turandot?
   (1 point for each correct answer, for a total of 4)

257. What is the name of Madame Butterfly's baby? (1)

258. What is the "secret" of Susanna? (3)

259. Who wrote the libretto for *Pagliacci*, composed by Leoncavallo? (2)

260. Who was the real-life poet who became the subject of a *verismo* opera? (2)

261. What is the name of the famous publishing house that published all Puccini's operas but one? (1) What was the one opera this house did not publish, and who did publish it? (4)

262. What conductor named his children after characters in Alfredo Catalani's operas? (2)

263. A great Italian actress made a powerful impression in a play by Giovanni Verga, which was later made into an opera.
(a) What is the name of the play and the opera?

(b) Who was the actress to first perform the work on the stage?
(2 each, for a total of 4)

Scene Six: Wagneriana

Three Tenors into Tristan *Don't Go*

264. Which three tenors sang Tristan during one performance at the Met? (6) Who was the thrice-blessed Isolde? (2)

265. What American soprano sang the first Elsa at Bayreuth? (2)

266. What famous singer lived in Lucerne in the house once occupied by Richard Wagner, which he named Triebschen? (4)

267. What is the name of Wagner's first opera? (2)

268. What was supposedly Wagner's favorite Italian opera? (3)

269. With the exception of George Bernard Shaw, Wagner did not find much favor with contemporary critics. What are the operas described by the following reviews:

(a) "It is poison—rank poison. All we can make out is an incoherent mass of rubbish, with no more real pretension to be called music than the jangling and clashing of gongs and other uneuphonious instruments with which the Chinamen, on the brow of a hill, fondly thought to scare away our English 'blue jackets!'" (*Musical World*, London, 1855.) (3)

(b) "Not merely polyphonous, but polycacophonous." (*Musical World*, London, 1855.) (3)

(c) "Reminds me of the old Italian painting of a martyr whose intestines are slowly unwound from his body on a reel." (Eduard Hanslick, 1868.) (3)

(d) "Where it is not silly, it is dirty. . . . Any half-hour of it . . . would make you blush if you had a . . . moral nature as tough as a section of New York pie-crust." (*Sunday Herald*, London, 1882.) (3)

270. It seems that the critics were not satisfied with excoriating Wagner; they used him to lash other composers. Name the opera masterpieces that were described by the following reviews:

(a) ". . . scarcely rises above the vulgarity of Offenbach. The orchestra is in the Wagnerian school, though it lacks the richness and flow of Wagner . . ." (Boston *Gazette*, 1879). (3)

(b) "So we get few set pieces or few prolonged melodies; indeed, the short bursts of sustained melody are generally formless. Here is the Wagner theory skeletonized, almost reduced to an absurdity." (New York *Sun*, 1901). (3)

(c) "The libretto is a compound of lust, stifling perfumes and blood, and cannot be read by any woman or fully understood by anyone but a physician . . . Meanwhile Wagner's Music of the Future has become the music of the past, and he is much too simple for the modern neurotic." (Boston *Daily Advertiser*, 1906). (3)

271. It wasn't only the critics who heaped abuse on Wagner. Name the celebrities who said the following:

THE WAGNER MUSIC-DRAMA IN NEW YORK—SCENE FROM "DIE WALKURE."—DRAWN BY T. DE THULSTRUP.—[SEE PAGE 119.]

(a) "Wagner's music is really better than it sounds." (2)

(b) "It may be that the Nibelungs' Ring is a very great work, but there has never been anything more tedious and more dragged-out than this rigmarole. . . . In the past, music was supposed to delight people, and now we are tormented and exhausted by it." (5)

(c) "Wagner is evidently mad." (5)

(d) "*Siegfried* was abominable. Not a trace of coherent melodies. It would kill a cat and would turn rocks into scrambled eggs from fear of these hideous discords. . . . The opening of the third act made enough noise to split the ears. . . ." (5)

272. Authors jumped on Wagner, also. What famous nineteenth-century novel contains these observations by a character?

"I like Wagner's music better than anybody's. It is so loud that one can talk the whole time without people hearing what one says." (5)

273. Who is the Swan in *Lohengrin?* (2)

274. What character from another Wagner opera is mentioned in *Lohengrin?* (2)

275. Who was the lady whose love affair with Wagner inspired *Tristan und Isolde?* (2)

276. What undisputed opera star always appears onstage but never sings a note? (5)

Wagner's Opera Quiz

277. In the *Ring of the Nibelungen,* Mime and Wotan (as the Wanderer) ask three riddles of each other, the loser to forfeit his head. Give the correct answers. (2 points for each correct answer, for a total of 12)

Mime's Questions:

(a) What is the race born in the earth's deep bowels?
(b) What race dwells on the earth's back?
(c) What race dwells on cloudy heights?

Wotan's Questions:

(a) What is the noble race which Wotan ruthlessly dealt with, yet deems most dear?
(b) What sword must Siegfried strike with to kill Fafner?
(c) Who can forge its broken pieces?

278. What work did Wagner write for the Philadelphia Centennial celebrations in 1876 for $5000? (2)

279. Which Wagnerian ladies would stymie even a medical examiner like Dr. Quincy if he had to determine the physical causes of their deaths? Name three for 5 points. (5)

280. What is the name of Brünnhilde's horse? (4)

281. Wagner was not the man to take all the abuse heaped on him by critics without fighting back. He took revenge in a devastating manner. Name the critic Wagner parodied in *Die Meistersinger*. (2)

282. Looking back, Wagner sometimes criticized his own work. Which opera did he describe as having "too much brass"? (2)

283. Name the three Rhinemaidens. (2 points for each Rhinemaiden, for a total of 6)

284. What is another opera based on the Nibelung legends beside the Wagner series? (3)

285. It was once commonly thought that Wagner's music killed the voice, and one singer may indeed have died due to the exhaustion of creating a leading Wagner role. Who was he and what was the opera? (4)

286. Name the first Wagner opera presented in the United States. (2)

Scene Seven: Ovations or Obscurity

This section is about opera composers and their works. Some of the composers mentioned in the quiz may be included here as well as in their own sections, so keep on your toes!

287. Who is the most famous singer to be portrayed in an opera? (6)

288. What are the three most famous operas based on the story *Manon Lescaut* by Abbé Prévost? (3)

289. What opera so impressed Beethoven that he kept it by his bedside and modeled *Fidelio,* his only opera, on it? Also give the name of the composer. (4)

290. How many versions of *Fidelio* did Beethoven write? (2)

291. How many overtures did Beethoven write for *Fidelio?* (3)

292. What opera features a deaf-mute in the leading role? (3)

293. What opera performance actually triggered a revolution? (2)

294. Name three opera composers who were the subjects of operas themselves. (4)

295. For *Der Rosenkavalier*, Richard Strauss used a "dynamite" waltz theme by another Strauss (no relation). Can you name this Strauss? (6)

296. The opera *Mignon* is based on what play by whom? (2)

297. Alfred Bruneau was a distinguished French composer whose operas *Messidor, L'Ouragan* and *L'Enfant-Roi* were set to libretti by an even more celebrated writer. Name him. (3)

298. What opera aria did Bizet appraise as "garbage"? (2)

299. Can you name five French operas that had achieved one thousand performances in Paris as of 1959? (6)

300. Who wrote the libretto for *Le Vaisseau Fantôme*, composed by Pierre-Louis Dietsch? (5)

301. What are the two standard repertory operas with music by Ernest Guiraud? (7)

302. What Massenet opera features the "Meditation"? (1)

303. What famous chorus did Gounod write for his *Ivan the Terrible*? (3)

304. Name the five Russian composers who were members of "The Five." (5)

305. Name the three composers of *Prince Igor*. (4)

306. Everyone knows about Serge Diaghilev's Ballets Russes, but did you know that his first stage presentation in the Western world was not a ballet but an opera? Name the opera and the star. (4)

307. Here are questions based on real-life family ties in the world of Russian opera, as submitted by Stanley Appelbaum.
(a) What famous Russian composer collaborated with his brother on the libretto of an opera considered his finest, an adaptation of a Pushkin short story? (3)
(b) In the world premiere of that same opera, what real-life husband and wife performed the two leading roles of the unhappy lovers? (3)
(c) Four operas by another well-known composer, in their world premieres, had major bass roles filled by the father of the composer's star pupil. Name the bass and the operas. (10)

308. The most famous Russian opera is *Boris Godunov*, by Modest Mussorgski. Who is the composer who adapted it into the version most often used? (1)

309. Name the composer who had an opera produced at the Vienna State Opera when he was only eleven years old. (2)

310. What romantic opera by a German composer was set to a libretto in English? (2)

311. This question was sent to us by Risë Stevens, longtime Met favorite who is now the executive director of auditions for the Metropolitan Opera National Council, and it's a tough one! For 10 points name ten Italian composers whose last names do not end with an *i*. (10)

312. Name six opera composers who stooped to the profession composers hate most by being *critics* themselves! (1 point for each, for a total of 6)

313. The writer Stendhal wrote a famous biography of Rossini. Can you name two other composers Stendhal wrote biographies of? (3)

314. Name the composer who rose 'from being a cook at court to a position of eminence in the world of music and politics. (4)

315. What signer of the Declaration of Independence also composed an opera? No bonus for deciding which was the braver feat! (9)

316. What nineteenth-century composer of *lieder* failed in his more than ten attempts to write a successful opera? (3)

317. Who composed what opera based on a daily newspaper report? (4)

318. Although many composers have surely thought it, only one said, "I gave no consideration to the singers at all." Who was the composer and what was the opera? (4)

319. Who was the first composer to live to see the one-thousandth performance of one of his operas? (5)

320. What famous writer composed an opera called *Undine?* (3)

321. What opera is the sequel to a popular one written by the same composer, even though the heroine dies at the end of the first work, and even though the titles of both operas incorporate the name of the heroine? (3)

The Bard in Opera

322. (a) We found nine operas based on Shakespeare's
        The Merry Wives of Windsor. For 10 points,
        name seven of their composers. (10)
    (b) We found ten operas based on Shakespeare's
        Romeo and Juliet. Take 10 points if you can name
        eight of their composers. (10)

323. What two composers wrote operas called:
(a) *The Barber of Seville*
(b) *Otello*
(c) *La Bohème*
    (2 points for each pair, for a total of 6)

324. Name an opera that features Napoleon as a leading
character. (2)

325. What sum is the bride bartered for in Smetana's *The
Bartered Bride*? (7)

326. Who begins an opera by singing the numbers
"5-10-20-30-36-43"? (2)

The Baritone's Lament

327. "The tenor always gets the girl!" Over the centuries,
this has been the complaint of baritones and basses (no one
listens to basses except the audience). And for the most part
it's true. But there are some operas in which the baritone
gets the girl. Name three. (2)

Opera Burial Plots

328. (a) What opera features a story in which: a mother is
        burned to death, a child is burned to death, a

woman is poisoned and a brother is beheaded? (2)
(b) Name two opera heroines who die from smelling flowers. (4)
(c) What opera heroine is killed by Jack the Ripper? (2)
(d) What opera, once called a shabby little shocker, features these grisly ingredients: torture, murder, shooting, knifing, suicide and double crosses? (2)
(e) What opera heroine dies from an overdose of jimsonweed? (3)
(A grisly total of 13 points)

329. The following real-life people became the subjects of what operas?
(a) Marie Duplessis
(b) King Gustavus III of Sweden
(c) Johann Christian Woyzeck
(1 point for each correct answer, for a total of 3)

Italian Opera Immigrants

330. (a) What Italian opera heroine dies on the shores of Louisiana? (2)
(b) Name at least two Italian operas that take place entirely in the United States. (3)

331. Although encores are now frowned upon during the performance of opera, there is one that cannot be avoided since it is part of the libretto. What is the opera in which one character asks another to repeat an aria? (3)

332. These famous operas have been presented in versions revised by eminent composers. Take 5 points if you can name all four of the "revisers."
(a) *Iphigénie en Aulide,* originally composed by Gluck.

(b) *Die Drei Pintos,* originally composed by Von Weber.
(c) *Idomeneo,* composed by Mozart.
(d) *Orfeo ed Euridice,* by Gluck. (5)

333. For 3 points, name at least two works for the lyric stage based on the legend of Pygmalion. (3)

Opera Literati

334. (a) Who was the highest-ranking ecclesiastic to write a libretto? (8)
  (b) Name the once-famous opera librettist who operated a still in America. (3)
  (c) Who signed his name to the libretto of what famous opera as Tobia Gorrio? (4)

335. What opera features a ballet danced by the ghosts of nuns who have broken their vows? (3)

336. What opera composer struck himself on the foot with his baton and died from gangrene of the injury? (4)

337. Can you identify the composer who was originally named Jakob Liebmann Beer? (2)

338. What opera character made his first literary appearance in a play called *El Burlador de Sevilla?* (4)

339. Who was the first woman to compose an opera? (6)

340. The following were all successful operas at one time. Can you name the composers of these works? (2 points each, for a total of 14)

(a) *I Gioielli della Madonna*   (c) *Fra Diavolo*
(b) *Die Königin von Saba*   (d) *Dinorah*

(e) *The Bohemian Girl*   (g) *Le Postillon de*
(f) *L'Amore dei Tre Re*   *Longjumeau*

341. While most famous opera arias derive their names from the opening sentence of the aria, like "Celeste Aida," "Vissi d'arte," "Un bel dì" and so on, many do not. For 2 points each, identify the following famous arias that begin:
(a) "Quando me'n vo' so-let-ta per la via . . ."
(b) "Fin ch'han dal vi-no, Cal-da la tes-ta . . ."
(c) "Mor-gen-lich leuch-tend im ro-si-gen Schein . . ."
(d) "Ah! Je ris de me voir si belle en ce mi-roir! . . ."
(e) "Là-bas dans la fo-rêt plus som-bre . . ." (10)

342. Prima donna Wilhelmine Schröder-Devrient was so impressive in *Fidelio* that a young student who saw her perform resolved to compose operas.
(a) Who was the student? (2)
(b) What operas did he compose that Schröder-Devrient sang in the premieres of? (3)

RICHARD WAGNER, COMPOSER OF THE "CENTENNIAL INAUGURATION MARCH."

ACT III: Answers

Scene One: Beginner's Luck: The Dawn of Opera

185. *Dafne* by Jacopo Peri was first performed in 1597.

186. Pietro Metastasio, the author of libretti that became the models for opera in the eighteenth century. Some individual works were set as many as seventy times by very famous composers, including Handel, Gluck, Mozart and Haydn. Mozart's *La Clemenza di Tito* was set to Metastasio's libretto.

187. Maggie Teyte.

188. (a) *Ercole Amante,* by Francesco Cavalli.
(b) Lully.
(c) *Xerse,* also by Cavalli.

189. *Alceste,* by Jean-Baptiste Lully.

190. George Frideric Handel *vs.* Giovanni Bononcini in London during the 1720s; Christoph Willibald von Gluck *vs.* Niccolò Piccini in Paris during the 1770s; Wolfgang Amadeus Mozart *vs.* Antonio Salieri in Vienna during the 1780s. The first two rivalries are almost forgotten, as are the composers who lost the struggles, Bononcini and Piccini, but the third rivalry has kept the name of Salieri alive and has been the subject of operas and plays, including the recent hit play *Amadeus.*

191. From 1752 to 1754 the "Guerre des Bouffons" (War of the Comic Actors) was a struggle over opera philosophy as represented by the old French school of Lully and Rameau

and the new Italian comic style as exemplified by Pergolesi's
La Serva Padrona. Supporters of Lully and Rameau were
known as the King's Corner and included the king and
Madame de Pompadour. Supporters of Italian Opera Buffa
were known as the Queen's Corner and included the queen,
Diderot and Rousseau. The war came to a silly end when the
director of the Opéra-Comique produced a comic opera in
French supposedly by an Italian. The Queen's Corner
gloated over its triumph only to choke on the revelation that
the opera, *Les Troqueurs*, had been written by a Frenchman
after all, Antoine d'Auvergne. Thus concluded a bloodless
battle that sounds more like an Offenbach operetta!

192. (a) Jean-Jacques Rousseau (1712–1778) composed the
famous *Le Devin du Village*.
(b) François André Philidor (1726–1795), who published a famous chess book, was a gifted composer
of popular operas.

193. Ranieri dé Calzabigi's libretti for Gluck's *Orfeo*,
Alceste and *Paride ed Elena* represented a return to sim-
plicity and naturalness from the excesses of *opera seria*.

194. The text is by John Gay, with an overture composed
by Dr. Johann Pepusch, who also arranged the sixty-nine-
odd popular tunes that made up this smash hit.

195. Caffarelli, a *castrato*.

196. *Rinaldo*.

197. *Orfeo ed Euridice*, composed in 1791.

198. Ludwig van Beethoven.

Scene Two: Mozart

199. Mozart wrote *La Finta Semplice*, which was nothing less than a full-fledged *opera seria*, in 1768, at the age of twelve. This immature work, by Mozart's standards, is not in the modern repertory, but his next effort, *Bastien and Bastienne*, written later that same year, is still performed and has been recorded several times.

200. (a) 2,065.
    (b) Donna Elvira.

201. As Da Ponte put it in his entertaining memoirs,

At night I shall write for Mozart and I shall regard it as reading Dante's *Inferno;* in the morning I shall write for Martín [y Soler] and that will be like reading Petrarch; in the evening for [Antonio] Salieri and that will be my Tasso.

Da Ponte worked especially hard "researching" *Don Giovanni.*

A beautiful young girl of sixteen was living in my house with her mother . . . (I should have wished to love her only as a daughter—but—) She came into my room whenever I rang the bell, which was fairly often, and particularly when my inspiration seemed to begin to cool. She brought me now a biscuit, now a cup of coffee, or again nothing but her lovely face, always happy, always smiling, and made precisely to inspire poetic fancy and brilliant ideas.

Considering the success of *Don Giovanni,* who can argue with Da Ponte's methods?

202. Here are four famous tenor Dons: Niccolò Tacchinardi, Mario, Manuel Garcia and Jean de Reszke. Take the points if you found any others as famous as the above.

203. *Die Zauberflöte* by Mozart and *Fidelio* by Beethoven. As manager of the Theater an der Wien, Schikaneder contracted for the opera first produced as *Leonore*. Earlier Schikaneder had commissioned Mozart to compose *Die Zauberflöte* to a libretto by Schikaneder himself.

204. Casanova, a genuine expert.

205. *Così fan Tutte* was commissioned because the Emperor Joseph was amused by a story of two men betting that each could seduce the other's "faithful" fiancée.

206. Michael William Balfe, composer of *The Bohemian Girl*, had an important career as a baritone in major European opera houses.

207. *Sethos,* a romance written in 1731 by Abbé Terrasson, and a great influence on eighteenth-century Masons.

208. *Così fan Tutte.*

209. Not Donna Elvira or Donna Anna, as you might think for a diva of such stature, but Zerlina, the soubrette part, which Patti made into a star part.

210. Irish tenor Michael Kelly, the composer of *Bluebeard,* was the first Don Basilio in *Figaro*. Ludwig Fischer, the fabled basso, composed "Im Tiefen Keller" to exploit his extraordinary deep voice, as had Mozart in the role of Osmin, which Fischer created.

211. *Die Zauberflöte.* It was based on *Lulu* by Liebeskind and of course bears no relationship to the opera composed by Alban Berg.

212. Susanna, despite Count Almaviva's amorous designs.

213. Müller's magic instrument was a zither. The success of his *Kaspar der Fagottist, oder die Zauberzither* prompted Mozart and Schikaneder to alter their already-started *Die Zauberflöte*. By 1818, however, the tables had been turned, and Müller cashed in on Mozart's success by producing a travesty of *Die Zauberflöte*.

214. "Rafaello!" exclaims his long-lost natural mother, Marcellina, as his natural father, Dr. Bartolo, watches with considerable surprise.

215. *Die Zauberflöte*. Giesecke was a minor member of the Schikaneder troupe who created a small role in the premiere of *Die Zauberflöte*. The author of several libretti, his claim was taken seriously by Otto Jahn and Edward J. Dent, two eminent Mozart authorities.

216. The third play was *La Mère coupable*. André Grétry once considered composing an opera based on it.

217. The "droit de seigneur" was the ancient custom by which the lord of a manor could sleep with any bride in his domain on the night she was married. This odious custom and others like it helped cause the French Revolution and is one of the reasons *Figaro* was such a dangerous play and opera politically.

218. *Fra Due Litiganti*, by Giuseppe Sarti; *Una Cosa Rara*, by Martín y Soler and *Le Nozze di Figaro* by Mozart.

219. Ironically, one teacher of Mozart's son was the man who confessed to be the composer's murderer, Antonio Salieri. The truth of Salieri's raving confession has never been proved or disproved, but most historians discount it. However, there is little question that Salieri did to Mozart's career and financial condition great harm, so his bad name is richly deserved.

220. *Zaïde*.

221. Aloysia Lange née Weber later became Mozart's sister-in-law when he married her sister Constanze. She created the role of Donna Anna for the Vienna premiere of *Don Giovanni*.

222. The 1940 revival of *The Marriage of Figaro*, which featured Ettore Panizza leading the dream cast of Ezio Pinza, Bidu Sayão, Elisabeth Rethberg, Risë Stevens and John Brownlee, which proves you just can't satisfy critics with quality.

223. When Ezio Pinza rang the doorbell for an interview for the part, Walter's normally dull, middle-aged cook came back gasping, "There's such a beautiful man outside!" convincing Walter that he had found the perfect Don.

Scene Three: Bel Canto Mad Scenes

224. Gioacchino Rossini.

225. *Poliuto*.

226. *The Barber of Seville*. Although *Barber*'s premiere was an unrelieved fiasco, it was not long before it became one of the favorite works in the repertory.

227. Lucia, Edgardo, Enrico, Arturo, Normando, Raimondo.

228. Gioacchino Rossini, *The Barber of Seville*.

229. Here are a few of them: *Lucia di Lammermoor, Anna Bolena, Linda di Chamounix, Maria Padilla, Parisina, Lu-*

*crezia Borgia, Il Furioso, Torquato Tasso, Maria Stuarda,
Roberto Devereux, Maria di Rudenz.*

230. The Barber of Seville is an itinerant barber and does not have a shop or a barber pole.

231. *Maria Stuarda.*

232. (a) *Adelson e Salvini.*
     (b) *Bianca e Fernando.*

233. Enrico Caruso, for his first Edgardo. Supposedly this was the first time in many years that patrons stayed beyond the mad scene!

234. Gilbert Duprez makes this assertion in his *Souvenirs d'un Chanteur.* The tenor was a close friend of Donizetti, and his claim must be taken seriously.

235. *Parisina.* The soprano is unfavorably compared to Malibran and Sontag.

Scene Four: Verdi

236. In his youth Arrigo Boito, composer of *Mefistofele,* was critical of Verdi, yet he wrote the libretti for *Otello* and *Falstaff* and revised *Simon Boccanegra.*

237. (a) Arturo Toscanini.
     (b) Sir Georg Solti.
     (c) Arturo Toscanini.

238. *Aida* was premiered in Cairo, Egypt.

239. The premiere of *Aida* was conducted by Giovanni

Bottesini, world famous as the foremost double-bass virtuoso of the day.

240. Antonio Ghislanzoni.

241. Francesco Maria Piave.

242. *Le Roi s'amuse.* Victor Hugo was not amused by the metamorphosis of his play into *Rigoletto*.

243. In later years this cry, of course, meant long life to the composer Giuseppe Verdi, but during the Italian drive for independence in the 1850s, the cry was a code for Vittorio Emmanuele *Re d' Italia*. Verdi's name was a convenient double entendre which the people used to escape the wrath of the law.

Scene Five: Puccini and the Other "Verists"

244. Maria Jeritza and Grace Moore were two blondes who had the looks to justify the decision.

245. *Gianni Schicchi* is based on Canto XXV and XXX of Dante's *Inferno*.

246. After an overexcited Scarpia knocked Maria Jeritza down during a rehearsal, she continued singing. Puccini loved the effect, and it has become traditional. Another famous Met Tosca, Geraldine Farrar, saw it differently and offered these choice observations in her autobiography *Such Sweet Compulsion*, published in 1938:

. . . the "clou" of the performance lay in a pose of unashamed abandon on the floor during the famous "Vissi d'Arte." From my seat, however, I obtained no view of any expressive pantomime on her pretty face, while I was surprised by the questionable flaunting of a well-cushioned and obvious posterior.

For the first time in his career, the wary Scotti was non-plussed by this act that completely spoiled his previous conception of attack on the defenseless heroine. With the lady writhing on the floor, there was nothing for him to do but stand, guardedly, against the wall . . .

247. Puccini sold a manuscript of "Musetta's Waltz" for three thousand dollars to an American millionaire in order to buy a motorboat when he came to America. No doubt he returned to Italy convinced that America's streets were paved with gold.

248. *La Fanciulla del West, Gianni Schicchi, Suor Angelica* and *Il Tabarro*. According to the Puccini biographer Howard Greenfeld, in *Puccini*, the composer did not consider the Met premiere of the *Trittico* to be the true world premiere.

While the *Trittico* was having its official world premiere in New York, Puccini busied himself with preparations for its first European presentation to take place at Rome's Teatro Costanzi on January 11, 1919. For him this was the real premiere, the first performance which would benefit by his supervision and careful attention.

249. (a) Cesira Ferrani.
   (b) She created both Mimi and Manon.
   (c) Rosina Storchio created *Butterfly* in its unsuccessful premiere.
   (d) Salomea Kruszelniski sang the first performance of the revised version.
   (e) Geraldine Farrar.
   (f) Tosca.

250. His first opera, *Le Villi,* was based on the same legend.

251. (a) David Belasco.
(b) Blanche Bates.

252. (a) Victorien Sardou.
(b) Maurice Barrymore, the father of John, Ethel and Lionel Barrymore, claimed Sardou stole the story from a scenario he had sent Bernhardt entitled *Nadjezda*.
(c) Sarah Bernhardt.

253. Giuseppe Giacosa and Luigi Illica.

254. *Madame Butterfly* flopped at its premiere at La Scala. The composer revised it successfully for its second premiere in Brescia, where it realized the popularity it still retains today.

255. Ferruccio Busoni.

256. (a) Hope.
(b) Blood.
(c) Turandot.
(d) Calaf asks Turandot to discover his name (so she can know she'll be Mrs. Calaf?).

257. Trouble.

258. The awful "secret" of Susanna in Ermanno Wolf-Ferrari's delightful *Il Segreto di Susanna,* premiered in 1909, is that she smokes.

259. Leoncavallo, a talented librettist. Puccini even considered him as a potential librettist for his own operas, although any possibility of that ended with the *La Bohème* feud, when Leoncavallo's intentions to write the opera were ignored by Puccini.

260. André Chénier, the real-life poet who was executed in the French Revolution, became Giordano's *Andrea Chénier*.

261. The House of Ricordi published all Puccini's operas except *La Rondine*, which was published by the House of Sonzogno.

262. Arturo Toscanini, a close friend of Catalani, named his children Wanda, Wally and Walter.

263. (a) *Cavalleria Rusticana*.
(b) Eleanora Duse.

Scene Six: Wagneriana

264. On December 28, 1959, the Met presented *Tristan* with a different tenor for each act. Ramon Vinay, Karl Liebl and Albert Da Costa were each one-third of Tristan to a whole Isolde, Birgit Nilsson. One wonders how many in the audience may have recalled, with more than nostalgia, the incomparable Lauritz Melchior, who had been in retirement for ten years.

265. Cosima Wagner's selection of Lillian Nordica, born in Farmington, Maine, to sing Elsa caused consternation in Germany regarding the passing over of native sopranos for the part. The consternation turned to cheers with Nordica's brilliant performance.

266. Minnie Hauk, who settled there with her husband, the Baron von Hesse-Wartegg.

267. *Die Feen,* which was not produced until 1888.

268. Bellini's *Norma*.

269. (a) *Lohengrin*.
    (b) *Tannhäuser*.
    (c) *Tristan und Isolde*.
    (d) *Siegfried*.

270. (a) *Carmen*, by Bizet.
    (b) *Tosca*, by Puccini.
    (c) *Salome*, by Strauss.

271. (a) Mark Twain.
    (b) Tchaikovsky (letter written in 1876).
    (c) Hector Berlioz (letter written in 1861).
    (d) Richard Strauss (letter written in 1879). Later Strauss repented this letter, calling his comments tomfooleries.

272. *The Picture of Dorian Gray,* by Oscar Wilde.

273. Elsa's brother, Duke Godfrey.

274. Parsifal. At the end of *Lohengrin* the knight declares he is the son of Parsifal.

275. Mathilde Wesendonck.

276. "The Evening Star" in *Tannhäuser*, to which Wolfram sings his beautiful aria.

277. The answers to Mime's questions:
    (a) The Nibelungen.
    (b) The Giants.
    (c) The Gods.

The answers to Wotan's questions:

(a) The Wälsungen.
(b) Siegmund's Sword ("Nothung," Needful).
(c) A fearless hero, who will also kill Mime. Mime is terrified by the last question and doesn't answer. Answering for him, Wotan predicts Mime's death.

278. *The American Centennial March.* You get what you pay for, and in this case Philadelphia became the owner of Wagner's most insignificant composition.

279. (a) Ortrud dies when Lohengrin gives her a nasty look.
(b) Elisabeth prays to die to redeem Tannhäuser, and she does.
(c) Isolde dies for no particular reason after singing the "Liebestod."

280. Grane. Brünnhilde is supposed to mount Grane at the end of *Götterdämmerung* and ride into the flames, but the too-often huge Brünnhildes have usually been kind and sensible enough to just walk with Grane into the flames. The radiant Marjorie Lawrence, a leading Wagnerian soprano of the 1930s, startled everyone at the Met by leaping onto her horse in true Walküre fashion.

281. The celebrated anti-Wagner critic and close friend of Brahms, Eduard Hanslick, was parodied as Beckmesser in *Die Meistersinger*. Beckmesser, originally named Hans Lick until Wagner got cold feet, is a ridiculous pedant who sticks dogmatically to old-fashioned music virtues.

282. *Lohengrin.*

283. Woglinde, Wellgunde, Flosshilde.

284. *Sigurd* by Ernest Reyer is the most famous, but there are also *Die Nibelungen* by Heinrich Dorn and *Gudrun* by Felix Draeske.

285. Ludwig Schnorr von Carolsfeld (1836–1865) died a month after creating Tristan. This did not encourage singers to sing Wagner's roles.

286. *Tannhäuser* in New York in 1859.

Scene Seven: Ovations or Obscurity

287. Without question the most famous singer to be portrayed in an opera is the legendary Orpheus of ancient Greek mythology. He has been the subject of countless operas from the beginning of operatic history, in works by Monteverdi, Gluck and Offenbach, among others.

288. *Manon Lescaut* by Daniel François Auber, *Manon* by Jules Massenet and *Manon Lescaut* by Puccini.

289. *Les Deux Journées,* composed by Luigi Cherubini. Cherubini was also admired by Haydn, who called him the greatest living composer.

290. Three versions.

291. Four overtures.

292. *La Muette de Portici (The Dumb Girl of Portici),* by Daniel François Auber.

293. *La Muette de Portici* was the catalyst of the Belgian revolt after a performance on August 25, 1830. The opera is based on historical events in Italy in the seventeenth century and tells the story of the Neapolitan fishermen's revolt against their tyrants.

294. We found five: Giovanni Pergolesi, Alessandro Stradella, Mozart, Salieri and E.T.A. Hoffmann.

295. He used the waltz "Dynamiden" by Josef Strauss.

296. *Wilhelm Meister*, by Goethe.

297. Emile Zola.

298. "The Toreador's Song" from *Carmen*.

299. Boieldieu's *La Dame Blanche*, Gounod's *Faust*, Thomas's *Mignon*, Charpentier's *Louise* and Bizet's *Carmen*.

300. Richard Wagner, who later used the same libretto for his own *The Flying Dutchman*. This was considered somewhat unethical, since Wagner had sold the rights to Dietsch, but ethics were never of much concern to Wagner.

301. The New Orleans–born Guiraud (1837–1892) composed the recitatives to *Carmen* and revised *The Tales of Hoffmann*.

302. *Thaïs*.

303. The "Soldier's Chorus" from *Faust*. Gounod first wrote it for his unfinished *Ivan the Terrible*.

304. César Cui, Alexander Borodin, Mili Balakirev, Modest Mussorgski, Nikolai Rimski-Korsakov.

305. Alexander Borodin is the principal composer, but Rimski-Korsakov and Glazunov rescored and adapted the opera.

306. *Boris Godunov*, with Feodor Chaliapin, in 1908.

307. (a) Petr Ilich and Modest Ilich Tchaikovsky wrote the libretto of *The Queen of Spades (Pikovya Dama)*.
(b) In the premiere of *The Queen of Spades* (1890),

Nikolai Figner played Herman and Medea Mei-Figner played Lisa.

(c) Fyodor Stravinsky, father of Igor, was in the premieres of *May Night* (1880), *The Snow Maiden* (1882), *Mlada* (1892) and *Christmas Eve* (1895), all by Rimski-Korsakov.

308. Nikolai Rimski-Korsakov.

309. *Der Schneemann* was composed by the eleven-year-old Erich Wolfgang Korngold.

310. *Oberon* by Carl Maria von Weber was set to a libretto by J. R. Planché.

311. Leoncavallo, Boito, Cilea, Giordano, Nono, Alfano, Cimarosa, Paisiello, Mercadante, Dallapiccola are ten of them. There are a few more, so if you named some of the others, take the points.

312. Hector Berlioz, Engelbert Humperdinck, Virgil Thomson, Wagner, Carl Maria von Weber, Claude Debussy.

313. The author of *The Red and the Black* also wrote biographies of Haydn and Mozart.

314. Jean-Baptiste Lully, assigned to the kitchen at court because of his clumsiness, rose to become the official composer of France and a favorite of Louis XIV.

315. Francis Hopkinson composed what is sometimes called the first American opera, *The Temple of Minerva*, produced in 1781.

316. Franz Schubert.

317. Paul Hindemith, *Neues vom Tage*.

H. Hofmann del.

Tob. Bauer sc.

Othello and Desdemona

BOSTON ESTES & LAURIAT

318. Richard Strauss, discussing *Salome*.

319. Ambroise Thomas was at the Opéra-Comique on May 13, 1894, for the one-thousandth performance of *Mignon*.

320. E. T. A. Hoffmann, a writer of bizarre short stories.

321. Massenet's *Manon* was followed by the less successful *Le Portrait de Manon*. Sentimentalists will be interested to know that des Grieux's nephew marries Manon's niece, who happens to look just like her aunt!

322. (a) *The Merry Wives of Windsor* by Karl Ditters von Dittersdorf.
        The Merry Wives of Windsor by Otto Nicolai
        The Merry Wives of Windsor by Peter Ritter
        Falstaff by Michael William Balfe
        Falstaff by Giuseppe Verdi
        Falstaff by Antonio Salieri
        Falstaff by Adolphe Adam
        Herne le Chasseur by François André Philidor
        Sir John in Love by Vaughan Williams
        At the Boar's Head by Gustave Holst
     (b) Jiři Benda, Charles Gounod, Pietro Carlo Guglielmi, Filippo Marchetti, Heinrich Sutermeister, Nicola Vaccai and Riccardo Zandonai all composed operas called *Romeo and Juliet*. Other operas based on *Romeo and Juliet* include *I Capuletti e i Montecchi* by Bellini, *Los Amantes de Verona* by Conrado del Campo and *Les Amants de Verone* by Richard d'Ivry.

323. (a) Giovanni Paisiello and Gioacchino Rossini.
     (b) Gioacchino Rossini and Giuseppe Verdi.
     (c) Ruggiero Leoncavallo and Giacomo Puccini.
     No composer likes to have his opera libretto used

again. Rossini was asked not to set *Il Barbiere*, since it would possibly harm the earlier work by Paisiello, which was a standard repertory opera at the time, and subsequently suffered by a cabal organized by friends of Paisiello. His opera, of course, won out, while Paisiello's has become obscure, but Verdi revenged Paisiello when his *Otello* drove Rossini's into obscurity. Puccini and Leoncavallo brought out *La Bohème* at the same time, and the composers feuded ever after.

324. *Madame Sans-Gêne*, by Giordano is the most famous.

325. Three hundred gulden.

326. Figaro, in *The Marriage of Figaro*.

327. There are more than you think. Here are five:

In *La Bohème* the tenor's girl dies, but Marcello, the baritone, is left with charming Musetta.

In *The Magic Flute* the tenor wins Pamina, but the baritone ends up with the sexy Papagena—a draw.

In *The Marriage of Figaro* the baritone ends up with the attractive Susanna, while Count Almaviva, also a baritone, keeps the beautiful Rosina. In this opera the tenor is a dolt!

In *Carmen* the baritone ends up with the girl, but the jealous tenor kills her! (Tenors just can't stand to lose to a baritone.)

In *Così fan Tutte* the tenor and baritone both win their girls.

328. (a) *Il Trovatore*
   (b) Selika in *L'Africaine* commits suicide by smelling a mancinilla blossom, and Adriana Lecouvreur dies from smelling poisoned violets.
   (c) Lulu.

(d) *Tosca*.

(e) Lakmé. The drug is not responsible for the coloratura dizziness of the Bell Song.

329. (a) *La Traviata*.
(b) *Un Ballo in Maschera*.
(c) *Wozzeck*.

330. (a) Manon, in *Manon Lescaut* by Puccini.
(b) Puccini's *La Fanciulla del West* takes place in the American West; *Un Ballo in Maschera* is set in Boston.

331. In Delibes's *Lakmé*, Nilakantha orders Lakmé to repeat the Bell Song in order to lure the Englishman who loves her to betray himself.

332. (a) Richard Wagner.
(b) Gustav Mahler.
(c) Richard Strauss. (Also Ermanno Wolf-Ferrari, who revised *Idomeneo* the same year.)
(d) Hector Berlioz.

333. *Pimmalione* by Luigi Cherubini; *Die schöne Galatea* by Franz von Suppé; *My Fair Lady* by Lerner and Lowe; *Il Pigmalione* by Donizetti (written at age nineteen and never produced); *Galathée* by Victor Massé; *Pimmaglione* by Giovanni Cimadoro.

334. (a) Giulio Rospigliosi, later Pope Clement IX, wrote, among others, the libretto for the first comic opera, *Chi soffre, speri*, to music by Marco Marazzoli.
(b) Lorenzo Da Ponte, as much a rogue as Don Giovanni or Figaro, was also known to steal books from Columbia University and then sell them back.

(c) Arrigo Boitò, who loved anagrams, signed *La Gioconda* as Tobia Gorrio.

335. *Robert le Diable*. At the first performance the dance featured the famous Marie Taglioni.

336. Jean-Baptiste Lully (1632–1687).

337. Giacomo Meyerbeer.

338. Don Giovanni.

339. Francesca Caccini, daughter of composer/singer Giulio Caccini, mentioned earlier as the first woman to sing coloratura roulades, also wrote *La Liberazione di Ruggiero* in 1625, making her the first woman to compose an opera.

340. (a) Ermanno Wolf-Ferrari (e) Michael William
    (b) Karl Goldmark   Balfe
    (c) Daniel François Auber (f) Italo Montemezzi
    (d) Meyerbeer (g) Adolphe Adam

341. (a) "Musetta's Waltz"
    (b) "The Champagne Aria"
    (c) "The Prize Song"
    (d) "The Jewel Song"
    (e) "The Bell Song"

342. Richard Wagner wrote a letter to Schröder-Devrient crediting his ambition to become a composer to her performances. She created Adriano in his *Rienzi*, Senta in his *Der Fliegende Holländer* and Venus in his *Tannhäuser*.

Score _____

CHARACTERS AND COSTUMES IN THE OPERA OF LA GRANDE DUCHESSE DE GEROLSTEIN, AS PRODUCED BY BATEMAN'S PARISIAN OPERA TROUPE, NEW YORK.

ACT IV

Light Opera and Operetta

Scene One: Gilbert and Sullivan

Answers on page 106.

343. What was the first operetta Gilbert and Sullivan collaborated on? (2)

344. What were the last two operettas Gilbert and Sullivan created together? (3)

345. What Gilbert and Sullivan role was created by someone related to two American presidents? (3)

346. What Gilbert and Sullivan opera was extensively "pirated" in America? (2)

347. Despite their status as British institutions, one of the popular Gilbert and Sullivan operas was actually banned for a while in England. Which one and why? (3)

348. What was the cause of the quarrel that broke up the Gilbert and Sullivan team after their string of successes? (3)

349. What Gilbert and Sullivan opera was supposedly inspired by the falling of a sword off a wall? (2)

350. What is the paradox that keeps young Frederic with the pirate band in Gilbert and Sullivan's *Pirates of Penzance?* (2)

351. Who is the only Gilbert and Sullivan character to appear in more than one opera? (4)

352. Which Gilbert and Sullivan opera is based on a poem by Tennyson? (3)

353. Which Gilbert and Sullivan opera satirizes Oscar Wilde? (2)

354. Joe Papp's lively revival of *The Pirates of Penzance* is not the first jazzed-up version of a Gilbert and Sullivan opera to hit Broadway. Name two jazz versions of *The Mikado* given with all-black casts in 1939. (2 points each, for a total of 4)

355. *Memphis Bound!* was a Broadway adaptation of which Gilbert and Sullivan work? (3)

356. What Gilbert and Sullivan work had its British premiere in Paignton, England? (3)

Cobbler, Stick To Your Last

357. The excellent advice, "Cobbler, stick to your last," has often been given to operetta composers who ventured into grand opera. Gilbert warned Sullivan against his grand-opera ambitions with the phrase, but Sullivan persisted with *Ivanhoe,* and the world lost the partnership of Gilbert and Sullivan.

(a) What famous opera composer who had had a bad experience in operetta warned Franz Lehar with the "cobbler" advice?
(b) What famous operetta composer who had failed in opera warned the successful operetta composer Reginald De Koven with the "cobbler" advice?
(Take 3 points for each, for a total of 6)

Scene Two: Offenbach, Johann Strauss, Jr. and Assorted Operettas

Offenbach's Opera Send-Ups

358. What Offenbach operettas contain allusions to or direct quotations from:
(a) *William Tell* by Rossini
(b) *La Favorite* by Donizetti
(c) *Les Huguenots* by Meyerbeer
(d) *Orfeo* by Gluck
    (2 points for each answer, for a total of 8)

359. When *La Vie Parisienne* was presented in New York on June 12, 1876, a famous conductor led the performance. Who was he? (3)

360. In Offenbach's *Tales of Hoffmann*, there are references made to an opera being performed next door to the tavern in which Hoffmann tells his stories. What is the opera? (5)

361. No family has dominated operetta like the Strauss family of "Waltz Kings."
(a) Can you name all five members of this dynasty? (10)
(b) Who was the other operetta composer whose name was spelled slightly differently? (2)

362. Match the following operetta stars to the works in which they created leading roles:

(a) Hortense Schneider   (1) *The Merry Widow*
(b) Mitzi Günther   (2) *The Grand Duke*
(c) Ilka Von Palmay   (3) *La Belle Hélène*
(d) Fritzi Scheff   (4) *Babette*

(3 points for each correct match, for a total of 12)

363. What famous operetta had its world premiere on a bill with a farce entitled *Cryptoconchoidsyphonostomata?* (8)

Scene Three: Broadway

364. Many people regard *Showboat* as the first true American opera. In any case, it was an opera company that first presented *Showboat* in a non-Ziegfeld production in America. This company has given *Showboat* no less than ten times since 1930. Take 8 points if you can name the company. (8)

365. For the first production of *Showboat*, Magnolia was supposed to be Elizabeth Hines and the first Joe was to be Paul Robeson. Who played these parts at the opening in New York on December 27, 1927? (3 points for each, for a total of 6)

366. Where did Paul Robeson first play Joe in *Showboat?* (2)

367. For *Sally*, Jerome Kern attempted to use a rejected song from an old show, only to see it rejected again, this time by Marilyn Miller as Sally. What was the song that finally ended up in *Showboat*, and who first sang it? (6)

368. What operas were burlesqued on the nineteenth-century American stage as:
(a) *Soldiers and Seville-ians* (3)
(b) *Ill-True-Bad-Doer* (1)

369. One "Fred de Gresac," who wrote the book for a Victor Herbert operetta called *The Enchantress*, was married to a very famous opera singer. Name the singer. (8)

370. For the opening night of *Over the River*, a 1912 Broadway hit musical, two famous divas were onstage as patrons of a café. One was Fritzi Scheff. Who was the other, equally glamorous, prima donna? (3)

371. The plot of Irving Berlin's musical *Watch Your Step* involved opera. Not only did the ghost of Verdi appear, but the second act took place in a famous opera house. What was the opera house? (3)

372. What fabled opera tenor made his American stage debut in a work called *Yours Is My Heart?* (4)

373. Who were the original creators of the title roles in Gershwin's *Porgy and Bess?* (3)

374. Who wrote the book for Leonard Bernstein's *Candide?* (2)

375. The Rodgers and Hart musical *On Your Toes* featured a landmark ballet called "Slaughter on Tenth Avenue." Can you name the ballerina who starred in this ballet, as well as its choreographer? (3)

376. The following Broadway musicals all boasted established opera stars. Can you name them for two points each?
(a) *Naughty Marietta* (2 stars, for 4 points)

(b) *Love's Lottery* (2)   (e) *Pipe Dream* (2)
(c) *Babette* (2)   (f) *Bravo Giovanni* (2)
(d) *Most Happy Fella* (2)   (g) *Fanny* (2)

377. What famous operetta was written because Victor Herbert refused to write one? (4)

378. Two lovely sopranos of the 1920s went from Broadway to the Met. Name them. (3)

379. Can you name the operetta based on a story called *Old Heidelberg?* (1)

380. *The Canterbury Pilgrims* (1917) and *Rip Van Winkle* (1920) were both presented at the Met.
(a) Can you name their composer?
(b) What was his famous operetta hit?
(2 points for each, for a total of 4)

381. *Beggar's Holiday* was a 1946 updating of *The Beggar's Opera* by what composer? (4)

382. In Philadelphia in 1911 an opera by Victor Herbert premiered. What was it called? Can you name the tenor who starred in that performance? (4 points each, for a total of 8)

383. What musical did Kurt Weill compose for Gertrude Lawrence? (2)

384. Who composed the 1936 Broadway musical *Johnny Johnson?* (2)

385. What famous operetta has been presented on Broadway under the following names: *The Merry Countess, A Wonderful Night* and *Champagne, Sec?* (5)

THE WEAKER SEX. VIII.

HE GOES TO THE PLAY, BUT FINDS IT IMPOSSIBLE TO BECOME INTERESTED IN THE PIECE.

AT THE OPERA.

HE FAILS TO TAKE A FRIENDLY INTEREST IN THE GREAT COMPOSERS.

ACT IV: Answers

Scene One: Gilbert and Sullivan

343. *Thespis*. Unfortunately, all the music from this is lost except for the chorus "Climbing over rocky mountain," later used in *The Pirates of Penzance*.

344. *The Grand Duke* and *Utopia, Ltd*.

345. Blanche Roosevelt (a relation of Theodore and Franklin) created Mabel in the world premiere of *The Pirates of Penzance*, in New York.

346. *H.M.S. Pinafore*. By the time Gilbert and Sullivan brought their version of *H.M.S. Pinafore* to America, there were *Pinafores* with all-children, all-women, all-men and any other variation of casts that enterprising managers could think of staging.

347. *The Mikado*. During the visit of the real-life emperor of Japan, the work was banned in England to avoid causing offense.

348. A carpet. Gilbert objected to the cost of a new rug for the Savoy theater; when Sullivan sided with D'Oyly Carte, it was all over.

349. According to Gilbert, *The Mikado* was born when a samurai sword in his studio fell, almost "snicker-sneeing" him!

350. Frederic, or "The Slave of Duty," was born on February 29 in a leap year. Alive for twenty-one years, he has only had five birthdays. Having been apprenticed to the pirates until his twenty-first *birthday,* he will have to wait until 1940 (the opera premiered in 1879) to be free. Fortunately Mabel promises to wait.

351. Captain Corcoran of *H.M.S. Pinafore* reappears in *Utopia, Ltd.* as Captain, Sir Edward Corcoran, K.C.B., of the Royal Navy. Sullivan quoted his famous "What never?" music, to the delight of the opening-night audience.

352. *Princess Ida.*

353. *Patience.* Before the American premiere of *Patience,* D'Oyly Carte cannily arranged an American tour for Oscar Wilde so the American public would be familiar with his eccentricities.

354. *The Swing Mikado* and *The Hot Mikado.*

355. *Memphis Bound!* was an adaptation of *H.M.S. Pinafore* in 1945. Another, *Hollywood Pinafore* in 1945, fared as poorly. Both shows were flops.

356. *The Pirates of Penzance,* although it is doubtful anyone would recognize it from the performance that was given. With makeshift costumes and little of the actual music, it was done strictly for copyright purposes. It was billed *The Pirates of Penzance or Love and Duty,* and of course its American premiere, subtitled *The Slave of Duty,* was the final version.

357. (a) Giacomo Puccini, whose *La Rondine* fared so poorly.
    (b) Sir Arthur Sullivan warned De Koven. It is a pity he did not take the advice himself.

Scene Two: Offenbach, Johann Strauss, Jr. and Assorted Operettas

358. (a) *La Belle Hélène;* (b) *La Périchole;* (c) *La Grande-Duchesse de Gérolstein;* (d) *Orphée aux Enfers.*

359. Jacques Offenbach himself conducted. The star was the New York favorite Marie Aimée.

360. *Don Giovanni.*

361. (a) Johann Strauss, Sr. ("Father of the Waltz"), and his sons: Johann Strauss, Jr. (composer of *Die Fledermaus*), Josef Strauss, Eduard Strauss (conductor) and Eduard's son, Johann Strauss III (conductor).
   (b) Oscar Straus (1870–1954) composed *The Chocolate Soldier.*

362. (a)—3; (b)—1; (c)—2; (d)—4.

363. *Trial by Jury* by Gilbert and Sullivan premiered on March 28, 1878. Also on the bill was Offenbach's *La Périchole.*

Scene Three: Broadway

364. The St. Louis Municipal Opera.

365. The first Magnolia was Norma Terris; the first Joe was Jules Bledsoe.

366. In London at the Theatre Royal, Drury Lane, in 1928.

367. "Bill," immortalized by Helen Morgan in *Showboat* in 1927.

368. (a) *Carmen*.

(b) *Il Trovatore* as presented by The Mastadon Minstrels in 1880. In what must have been an amusing production, the villain was called Count Di-Loony!

369. "Fred de Gresac" was *Mrs*. Victor Maurel!

370. Geraldine Farrar.

371. The Metropolitan Opera House. The famous old auditorium was reproduced onstage, including the Diamond Horseshoe and a production on the opera stage. Actually the Met wasn't so old when *Watch Your Step* was produced in 1914.

372. Richard Tauber, in 1946. *Yours Is My Heart* was the Broadway name for Lehar's *The Land of Smiles*. He had first appeared in New York in 1931 in a song recital.

373. Todd Duncan was Porgy and Ann Brown was Bess.

374. Lillian Hellman.

375. Tamara Geva starred in the ballet choreographed by her husband, George Balanchine.

376.

(a) Emma Trentini and Orville Harrold	(d) Robert Weede
	(e) Helen Traubel
(b) Ernestine Schumann-Heink	(f) Cesare Siepi
	(g) Ezio Pinza
(c) Fritzi Scheff	

377. *The Firefly* (1912) by Rudolf Friml was written as a follow-up to Herbert's *Naughty Marietta* for Emma Trentini. After Herbert quarreled with Trentini, swearing never to write a note for her again, impresario Oscar Hammerstein I was fortunate to come up with the then-unknown Rudolf Friml and the immensely successful *Firefly*.

378. Mary Lewis and Grace Moore, who both debuted at the Met in Puccini's *La Bohème*.

379. *The Student Prince*, by Sigmund Romberg.

380. (a) Reginald De Koven; (b) *Robin Hood*. (1920)

381. Duke Ellington.

382. *Natoma*, starring John McCormack.

383. *Lady in the Dark* (1941).

384. Kurt Weill.

385. *Die Fledermaus* by Johann Strauss, Jr. Another famous production was *Rosalinda*, starring Dorothy Sarnoff. It was conducted by Erich Wolfgang Korngold.

Score _____

THE PRIMO TENORE.

(*Opera of "Maritana."*)

CURTAIN CALL

An encore of odd facts and questions. Answers on page 119.

386. What opera soprano sued a pasta factory? (2) (Hint: It was not Giuditta Pasta!)

387. Name the first American president to attend an opera performance. (2)

388. What is surely the most expensive opera recording of all time (if figured by cost to the buyer per minute of recording)? (4)

Opera Fiction

389. (a) Who wrote *The Phantom of the Opera?* (1)
  (b) There were three different movies, each with a different Phantom. Name two who played them. (3)

390. Toscanini walked out of many theaters in disgust, but returned later to most of them. However, there was one he refused to go back to unless he could "conduct on its ashes." Name the theater. (2)

391. What was the nineteenth-century English literary

character based on the very real singer Anna Bishop, wife of Sir Henry Bishop? (3)

392. What famous opera was composed for a girls' school? (3)

393. What opera is dedicated to all "The Beautiful Women of Milan"? (9)

394. What enormously famous nineteenth-century song was introduced in the opera *Clari, or The Maid of Milan?* Who wrote the words for this song? (2 points for each, for a total of 4)

395. What does *Anna Bolena* have in common with *Clari, or The Maid of Milan?* (4)

396. The Irish ballad "The Groves of Blarney" showed up as what famous aria in what opera? (5)

397. What famous folk song is incorporated into *Sir John in Love,* composed in 1929? (3)

398. What opera was parodied on the nineteenth-century American stage as *The Roof Scrambler?* (2)

399. Can you identify the literary classic on which all the following operas are based, for 4 points?
Fatme, by Benno Bardi; *La Statue,* by Ernest Reyer;
Gulnara, by Julia Weissberg; *The Barber of Bagdad,* by Peter Cornelius; *Mârouf,* by Henri Rabaud. (4)

400. When John Quincy Adams was defeated for reelection to the presidency, he would quote the lines "*Ô Richard! L'Univers t'abandonne.*" Can you identify the popular opera this passage comes from? (7)

401. What Italian opera did actor David Garrick's play *The Clandestine Marriage* become? (3)

402. What famous opera impresario invented a coffee drink that is still popular today? (4)

Strange Locations

403. (a) What opera features an aria sung in a bathtub? (7)
(b) What opera features a proposal of marriage sung from a phone booth? (2)

404. What opera features the reincarnation of one of the most famous portrait subjects in history? (3)

405. What 1838 opera features the literary precursor of Dracula? (2)

406. George Bernard Shaw wrote that two arias were worthy of being sung by the Almighty. Can you name them? (2)

407. The turn-of-the-century hit play, *Captain Jinks of the Horse Marines*, features the role of an opera soprano named after a city in New Jersey. Name the character and the city she is named after. (4)

408. Can you give the original title of the opera that had such a huge success in Paris as *Robin des Bois?* (4)

409. The ballad "El Arreglito," by Yradier, also the composer of the popular "La Paloma," was used for the entrance of a famous opera heroine. Can you name her? (2)

410. Opera, of course, wasn't always on the radio or television. There were several breakthroughs that led to the

riches we enjoy on the matinee broadcasts and PBS telecasts:
(a) Who was the star of the first radio broadcast of an opera from the Metropolitan Opera House? (4)
(b) Where did the first opera telecast originate from? (7)
(c) What was the first opera to be telecast from the Met? (2)
(d) Name the first opera expressly *commissioned* for radio. (10)
(e) Name the first opera to be *premiered* on radio. (10)
(f) What was the first opera expressly written for television? (2)

411. Opera made it into the movies early in the game:
(a) What opera diva starred in some of Cecil B. De Mille's *silent* movie epics? (2)
(b) What is the name of the movie featuring Conchita Supervia? (3)
(c) What is the name of the movie based on *La Bohème*, starring Jan Kiepura and Martha Eggerth? (4)
(d) Who composed an original opera for the movie *Give Us This Night?* (5)
(e) Who composed an original opera for the movie *Charlie Chan at the Opera?* (6)
(f) Who starred in the movie version of *Louise?* (1)
(g) Many operas have been adapted from stage plays, but we found only one opera based on an original movie, and a silent movie at that. We'll give you 20 points if you can name either the opera or the movie it was based on. (20)

412. Here are some questions based on recent movies.
(a) What diva starred in the movie of Harold Robbins's *The Adventurers?* (3)
(b) What basso played a mafia godfather in a Burt Reynolds film? (4)
(c) The Mother Abbess in the smash hit film *The Sound of Music* was played by Peggy Wood. Can you name her vocal instructor? (7)

(d) What opera tenor made a film of the life of the famed nineteenth-century tenor Gayarre? (5)

(e) Who sang the music of Emile de Becque in the movie of *South Pacific*? (4)

413. We asked you in the introduction to this book if you knew three operas. By this time, hopefully, you do. But do you know your opera *abc*'s?

For a bonus of 35 points, name twenty-six operas, each beginning with a different letter of the alphabet. Note: articles such as *La*, *Der*, *The* and the like do not count.

For example: *Aida*, *La Bohème* and *Carmen* are everybody's *abc*'s. (*La Bohème* counts for *b* and not *l*!)

Now you're on your own! To make it even tougher, don't use our *a*, *b* and *c* examples. (35)

HOOPS AT THE OPERA.

Usher. "No. 99, Sir?   There it is; a Good Seat, too, Sir!"

AT THE OPERA.

"That, Madam, is your Se.., and there is yours, Sir."

Curtain Call: Answers

386. Maria Callas, who else?

387. Although few presidents of the United States have been enthusiastic opera fans, the first one, George Washington, set a good example by going to a ballad-opera at the John Street Theater in New York in 1789. It is not reported whether Martha had to drag him there kicking and screaming.

388. The five-minute, one-sided record issued by Victor of the "Lucia Sextette" featuring Caruso, Sembrich, Scotti, Journet, Daddi and Severina sold in 1912 for $7. Not even allowing for inflation, a typical LP recording of opera highlights would have to sell today for $350 at that rate!

389. (a) Gaston Leroux.
    (b) Lon Chaney was the first, Claude Rains the second and Herbert Lom the third.

390. The Metropolitan Opera. For some reason Toscanini had a singular hatred for this institution. No completely satisfactory explanation has been given for his attitude or even for why he left it in 1915.

391. Anna Bishop was the model for Trilby, the soprano who is mesmerized by Svengali. Mrs. Bishop (1810–1884) left her husband, Sir Henry, to run off with her Italian instructor, harpist Robert Bochsa. They toured together, and she had a very successful career as a diva.

392. *Dido and Aeneas* by Henry Purcell in 1689, first performed at Mr. Josias Priest's Boarding School at Chelsey.

393. *L'Elisir d'Amore,* by Donizetti.

[119]

394. "Home Sweet Home." The words were written by the American actor John Howard Payne. The music was by Sir Henry Rowley Bishop.

395. *Anna Bolena* contains the melody of "Home Sweet Home."

396. "The Last Rose of Summer," in *Martha* by von Flotow.

397. "Greensleeves."

398. The immensely popular nineteenth-century opera *La Sonnambula* by Vincenzo Bellini was parodied by William Mitchell as *The Roof Scrambler* at the Olympic Theater in New York in 1839.

399. *The Arabian Nights*.

400. *Richard Coeur-de-Lion* by Grétry. It is a shame that this superb French opera is not better known today. Full of melody and charm, it would lend itself to a stunning production, and at one time was possibly the most popular opera in the world.

401. *Il Matrimonio Segreto*, by Cimarosa.

402. "Prince of Impresarios" Domenico Barbaja (1778–1841) was instrumental in the careers of Rossini, Bellini and Donizetti. He is credited with the invention of whipped cream on coffee or hot chocolate, known as *barbaiata*.

403. (a) *Transatlantic*, composed in 1930 by George Anthiel.
    (b) *The Telephone*, by Gian Carlo Menotti.

404. *Mona Lisa*, by Max von Schillings.

405. *Der Vampyr* (1828), by Heinrich Marschner, based on the story of Lord Ruthven by John Poldori.

406. The bass arias from *Die Zauberflöte:* "O Isis und Osiris" and "In diesen heil'gen Hallen."

407. Madame Trentoni, after the state capital of New Jersey, Trenton, was immortalized by Ethel Barrymore in her first starring role.

408. *Der Freischütz,* in a distorted translation by Castil-Blaze in 1824. The Romantics, including Victor Hugo, were in ecstasy, and the opera ran for 327 straight performances, reminding us that opera was once *the* popular entertainment.

409. Carmen, in Bizet's opera, enters to the "Habanera" taken from Yradier's "Arreglito."

410. (a) *I Pagliacci* was first broadcast from the stage of the Met on January 13, 1910, starring Enrico Caruso. This experimental broadcast was received by over fifty radio pioneers in New York City and the surrounding areas, as well as at sea by the S.S. *Avon.*

  (b) From Radio City, with a Metropolitan cast on March 10, 1941. The opera was, again, *Pagliacci.*

  (c) *Otello,* on opening night, November 29, 1948.

  (d) *The Willow Tree,* by Charles Wakefield Cadman, was commissioned by NBC and performed on October 3, 1933.

  (e) Charles Skilton's *Sun Bride,* on April 17, 1930.

  (f) Menotti's *Amahl and the Night Visitors,* first performed on Christmas Eve on NBC in 1951.

411. (a) Geraldine Farrar. In such movies as *Carmen* and *Joan the Woman,* Farrar became a genuine movie star. She was given the most lavish treatment accorded any star up to that time, traveling to Hollywood by private railroad car, for which she was paid by the mile!

(b) *Evensong*, an awful movie based on the life of Nellie Melba. Supervia is electrifying in the part of Baba L'Etoile! Who thought of that name?

(c) *The Charm of La Bohème*, another stupid movie. In this one the heroine conveniently dies at the end of the opera *La Bohème*, for real. This crazy play within the play is capped off by the heroine's father comforting her lover with the words, "She couldn't have had a better exit!"

(d) Erich Wolfgang Korngold.

(e) Oscar Levant. The baritone is played by Boris Karloff!

(f) Grace Moore. Supervised by the composer, Gustave Charpentier, it is one of the finest opera films ever made.

(g) *The Cheat*, released by Paramount in 1915, was the source for Camille Erlanger's opera *Forfaiture*, Paris, 1921.

412. (a) The beautiful Anna Moffo.

(b) Giorgio Tozzi plays a "don" in *Shamus*. An offbeat choice, Tozzi gave an excellent performance which would not discredit Marlon Brando.

(c) Emma Calvé.

(d) Alfredo Kraus.

(e) Giorgio Tozzi.

413. Here are our twenty-six:

Alceste (Gluck, Lully, etc.)   *Le Nozze di Figaro*
Il Barbiere di Siviglia   *Orfeo ed Euridice*
Cavalleria Rusticana   *Porgy and Bess*
Don Giovanni   *Queen of Cornwall* (Boughton)

Elektra	*Rigoletto*
Fidelio	*La Serva Padrona*
Die Götterdämmerung	*Tosca*
Les Huguenots	*Undine* (Hoffmann)
Idomeneo	*La Vestale*
La Juive	*Die Walküre*
Die Königskinder	*Xerse* (Cavalli)
Lucia di Lammermoor	*Yeomen of the Guard*
Manon	*Die Zauberflöte*

Like us, you probably had trouble with *q*, *x* and *y*, so we'll give you some of the other titles that would be acceptable as answers:

Q   *Quentin Durward*
      Quinto Fabio
      Quo Vadis
      (*Queen of Spades* doesn't count, since the title actually begins with P—*Pikovya Dama*)

X   *Xacarilla*
      Xavière
      Xerxes (We'll accept Handel's *Xerxes*, since it's so widely used, although actually the title begins with S—*Serse*)

Y   We hope you thought of Gilbert and Sullivan's *Yeomen*, but if not, you might like to know that two composers are responsible for:
      Yvrogne corrigé (Laruette in 1759, Gluck in 1760)

Evaluation

0 to 100 points:	Level 1—*Critic*. This profession requires least information about the subject.
101 to 1000 points:	Level 2—*Opera Manager*. Takes a little more knowledge.
1001 to 1914 points:	Level 3—*Opera Expert*.
1915 points:	Level 4—*Opera Book Author*. Only a perfect score entitles you to be the author.